CAPTAIN SCOTT MOORE'S SNOOK FISHING SECRETS

by G. B. Knowles

with Scott K. Moore

ISBN—0-9642942-0-6

Library of Congress 94-96379

Published by:

SEVEN PINES PUBLISHING COMPANY
P.O. Box 14069
Bradenton, Florida
34280-4069

Second Edition

Printed in the United States of America

This book is dedicated to my aunt, Henrietta Padgett, who always encouraged me to make a career of writing -- and to Albert R. and Janette Moore who took the time to take their young son fishing -- and started all this business.

CONTENTS

ACKNOWLEDGMENTS

Scott and I would both like to offer our deepest thanks to the many people who have made this book possible -- and for their help in other ways through the years.

Thanks to Frank Sargeant, Herb Allen, Jeff Klinkenberg, Rip Cunningham, Whit Griswold, Lefty Kreh, Vic Dunaway, Karl Wickstrom, Biff Lampton, both Colin Moore's, Jerry Hill, Steve Gibson, Lynn Mathews, Del Milligan, Jim Hardee, Don Moore, Larry and Lilliam Larsen, Jan Fogt, Mel Berman, Rusty Chinnis, Larry Mendez, Tom McEwen, Jack Elka, Van Hubbard, Captain Dale Marler, Bill Lowman, Pete and Bill Turner, Randy Edwards and the entire staff of Mote Marine Laboratory, Dennis Hart, Byron Stout, Phil Allessi, Andy Massaro, Jim Britt, Chris Mitchell, Jim O'Neill, Bob Bowden, Salty Sol Fleishman, Boyd Pfeiffer, Mark Weintz, Gaylord Carney and the entire crew of Film Works in Bradenton for their extreme patience. And thanks also to Kathy Odom for her special inspiration, and to Theresa Gianquinto for providing calm in the middle of a storm.

Special thanks also go to Ron Taylor and Mike Tringali of the Florida Marine Institute and Phil Chapman of the Florida Game and Freshwater Fish Commission -- the "father of snook hatcheries."

Extra special thanks go to Patti Knowles for computer help above and beyond the call of duty when our machines broke down at a critical time. Kudos also to Jim Knowles for his faith and counsel, and to Dona Vanderipe for her editing efforts. And many thanks to Jack, Bruce and George Manson for their generosity with Seven Pines.

And we greatly appreciate the efforts of Bob "Doc" Sammons, Brian Shaffer and Mitchell Rickey without whose help and encouragement this book would not have been possible.

I'm sure we've left somebody out by accident, but there are three men we would also like to demonstrate our appreciation and affection for. Thanks to the late Bill Hallstrom who bought my first story and gave me some encouragement when it was much needed. And Scott and I both owe a great debt to the late Sam Crosthwait and the late Frank Cavendish -- two men who were never too busy to teach a young boy how to catch a fish. More men need to do that.

As this book was about to go to press another tragedy took the life of a man that Scott and I have both enjoyed fishing with.

Nicholas Byrne was one of the finest of outdoor companions, and he was especially proud of his Irish heritage. So I would ask God and any Celtic saints up there to allow him one brief glimpse of this book. I know he would like it.

And may we one day --- on some spiritual stream --- finally be allowed to solve the question of which is the greatest of gamefish --- the Atlantic salmon that Nick adored, or the snook he adopted during our wonderful adventures together.

COVER: Tailwalking snook photograph by ***G. B. Knowles***

COVER DESIGN: ***Technical Art & Communication Corp.***

INTRODUCTION:

Captain Scott Moore is widely recognized as the finest snook fishing guide in the world. Captain Moore's praises have been sung in scores of magazine articles and newspaper stories. And Moore has been the chief inspiration for several books and videos.

Many consider Moore to be the best saltwater fishing guide in the United States. His exploits with tarpon, trout and redfish are on par with his snook fishing expertise. But it is Moore's knowledge of snook that elevates this guide to legendary status. Moore was the first fishing guide in the nation to guarantee snook catches. As such he has inspired and created a unique guide industry and transformed lazy snook fishing afternoons into what is today's most popular form of recreation in Florida -- the nation's fourth largest state.

If imitation is the sincerest form of flattery then there are many who recognize Moore's greatness. When Scott Moore started out in the charterboat business there were but a handful of inshore guides in the gulf of Mexico. Today there are hundreds. This book will not only tell the story of that transformation -- with Moore and the snook intricately linked to it -- but will share the snook fishing secrets of this master for the first time.

And there is but one writer who could tell this story. G. B. Knowles has won more than a dozen writing awards for his work over the years. Knowles has written for more than 20 newspapers and over a dozen national magazines. Knowles has also done outdoor radio and television work. But more importantly, Knowles and Scott Moore have been close friends since childhood. They have fished together for so long that Knowles understands many of Scott Moore's secrets by intuition alone. He has now used his writing talents to translate those secrets onto the written page.

Both Moore and Knowles live on the water firmly in the midst of snook country -- the grass flats adjacent to Tampa Bay, and Charlotte Harbor. Both of them regularly catch snook, literally, in their backyards -- often on small streamer flies.

Other books and articles have touched upon Moore's magic, but this is Captain Scott's book. It has been long in the planning and making. This book will help you catch more snook, trout, redfish, cobia, tarpon and freshwater gamesters like bass. But, it will also show you just why the snook is such a special fish.

We hope you enjoy it.

ABOUT THIS BOOK

AUTHOR'S NOTE: Scott Moore and I have known each other for a long time, since we were children. We attended Jessie P. Miller Elementary School in Bradenton, Florida together. So I guess we've known each other since about age six.

Consequently, Scott's story and mine have been intertwined over the years. As a young outdoor writer I had the privilege of being the first journalist to write about Scott Moore's snook catching abilities on a national level. At the time neither Scott nor I had any idea of the phenomenon we were creating. That was long before Scott Moore thought about becoming a fishing guide. We fished for fun back in those days.

In the 1970s only a handful of anglers successfully fished for snook, even though everybody wanted to catch the mystical linesider. In the 1990s thousands of people crowd the waterways chasing snook. And fishing for this ebony-striped gamester is one of the fasting growing forms of recreation in the U.S.

Scott and I began planning this book six or seven years before we sat down to publish it. But we did not really know how to go about doing it then. Originally we looked for a national publisher and thought about doing a book on general fishing in order to appeal to a national audience.

But things have changed so rapidly in the fishing and publishing worlds that our plans for this book also changed. By 1990 the regional publishing business -- at least in non-fiction -- was beginning to outstrip the big national publishing houses.

Meanwhile, saltwater snook fishing is rapidly approaching the appeal that largemouth bass fishing enjoys in freshwater. Consequently, the demand for information about the snook has skyrocketed across the nation. During the 1992-93 fishing season more than 122,000 snook stamps were sold in the state of Florida alone. And that doesn't count the snook anglers who fish with guides and don't need to purchase licenses. Nor does it include the close-mouthed anglers in south Texas who may encounter linesiders in the southern reaches of Laguna Madre. And, of course, there are thousands of armchair snook anglers in Maine or Montana who dream of one day doing battle with the tropical snook. The snook is a fish made for dreams.

Also, the snook occupies a warm place in both my heart and Scott's heart. Both of us realized that there are still huge misconceptions about this animal. None of the literature published on snook in the past, including the scientific papers, really had a complete handle on *Centropomus undecimalis*.

Even the stories I have written about Scott over the years have been guilty of certain omissions. If you read the chapter called TIGHT LIPS FOR TOMORROW you will understand why such omissions have been necessary in the past, and why we are pulling the gloves off in this book -- for the first time.

This is the complete story of the snook, modern snook fishing and the man, who not only single-handedly created modern snook fishing; but a man who, in my opinion, has done more to save the snook for the future than any other.

Although I didn't agree with him I couldn't have been more proud of Scott then at the first Snook Symposium when he urged lawmakers to close snook fishing. After all, here was a guy who made a living catching snook asking to be put out of business. It was a rare gesture of selflessness and one that demonstrates Scott Moore's passion for the creature we call the snook.

It was Scott Moore -- alone -- who showed scientists where and how to catch snook for research. And while many of those projects have failed for various reasons, the growing body of knowledge about snook adds to the popularity of the fish, and secures its future.

Largemouth bass are probably the most popular gamefish in the world. Consequently, they are also one of the most successful. The catch and release fishery that has colored bass fishing in the last quarter century is a direct result of the largemouth's popularity. And that has led to its success as well.

Scott and I see the same thing happening with snook, a fish I often refer to as the saltwater bass.

Yet snook are much harder to catch than bass, or any other sportfish. There are so many factors which change things for the snook that figuring out how to catch them is one of fishing's greatest challenges. So Scott and I believe that this book will appeal not just to linesider devotees, but to all anglers.

If you can master snook, then catching bass, or crappie, will be easy. Scott and I hope that will be much of the allure of this project. Savvy bass anglers should want this book as much as snook fishermen.

We have tried to tell an interesting story about Scott, the birth of modern snook fishing, the evolution of modern snook fishing and the life of *Centropomus undecimalis* itself.

There are five species of snook, yet this book will confine itself to *undecimalis* alone. If you can catch this large member of the snook tribe, in places where he has no business being, then nabbing his smaller cousins will be easy. Besides, the fat, swordspine and tarpon snook are rare in the U.S. and so small that most anglers don't care to target them. The large black snook of the Pacific coast has a limited range and is only available to traveling anglers.

In telling a complete story about the snook we have tried to explain when the best times to catch this fish will be, on different baits and lures. We think this is a complete book that demands thorough reading. However, we have arranged it in such a way that it can be used as a reference book as well. In that manner, a freshwater angler who wants a tip to help him catch more bass can study the chapter on TEN FISHING SECRETS and greatly up his take of largemouths.

Artificial lure devotees will find information on using lures and flies in: WINTER FISHING, TRANSITION FISHING, LIGHT TACKLE TACTICS FOR BIG FISH and in CATCHING SNOOK IN DEEP WATER. We cover fly and lure use throughout the book as well. But those chapters offer additional opportunities for anglers to learn how to fool fish with phony baits.

Live bait anglers will find a chapter on catching and using bait. But, then, this entire book revolves around the ancient relationship between the snook and his food sources.

Tips and secrets are scattered throughout the book. But, perhaps, the most important chapter is the one called LIVING ON THE EDGE. By reading this chapter you will begin to get a feel about just what being a snook means. And knowing him, thus, is important to catching him.

We hope you read the entire book, and enjoy it. But, if you can't find the time, you will find chapters that will appeal to your particular, individual angling style. If chasing snook from piers is your bag there's a chapter for you. If your goal is fly fishing for largemouth bass this book will make you more successful at that as well.

Regardless of your game, we hope this book will make fishing more enjoyable. And part of that will be catching more fish -- and understanding why you did.

G. B. Knowles
Seven Pines, Florida
May 26, 1994

Chapter 1

THE PRIMADONNA

Scott Moore and the snook have had a long history together. The love affair began on a dock near Saint Petersburg, Florida when an eight-year-old urchin called Scotty Moore caught his first linesider and demonstrated what is now known as the Scott Moore magic.

Young Scotty did not offer that snook a live pilchard or a carefully crafted lure. Instead the youngster tempted that first snook with a chunk of hot dog -- forever proving the old saw that 10 percent of the fishermen catch 90 percent of the fish.

We might say it was a portent of great things to come. We might argue that superior presentation of the hot dog and careful stealth enticed the linesider to gulp down that unusual bait. But there is more to it then that. Scott Moore understands fish in a manner few humans are capable of. Moore knows them viscerally. He feels the things they feel. He understands the subtleties of wind and tide and lunar phase that change a situation for the snook. And those factors -- more than anything else -- are the things that makes Scott Moore unique, even among fishing guides.

One story Moore tells illustrates just how much command he enjoys over the often puzzling marine environment. Scott had booked a client who had fished earlier with another guide. And the other guide had complained that this client was the kind who used a guide as a means of finding a good spot to fish. The client had returned in his own boat and was parked in the hole the guide had shown him the next day.

And, of course, that meant that the guide, with paying customers on board, was deprived of fishing a hole that he had discovered.

"But that didn't bother me," Scott says. "I took the guy to a place and caught him 40 snook. But it was a place that he would not be able to go back to for 14 days. By then he'd figured the fish were gone. And on that next moon I was fishing those snook again. And we caught all we wanted."

This two-man limit was indicative of the kind of catches that propelled Scott Moore to legendary status during the 1970's.

Those kinds of instincts are what led a small boy to conquer his first snook with a mere hot dog for bait. But being a fishing legend involves more than simply great talent. Luck counts as well. And Scott has enjoyed some degree of luck. Much of it was growing up at the right time with the right people.

Scott grew up in what was, then, the wilds of the Florida town of Bradenton. Forests and streams adjoined his home. Meanwhile, a number of old shell pits and lakes held trophy-sized largemouth bass. And one small pond was home to a lost but venerable tarpon of about 40-pounds.

Scott was boyhood friends with G. B. Knowles. And that brought him into contact with saltwater and snook. Each day after school Scott would ride his bicycle to his friend's home. Knowles lived on the shores of the Manatee River and the entire stretch of the river was his backyard. There Moore and Knowles whiled away the hours catching crabs, trout, redfish, snook and whatever else the river offered up. There the two cemented a mutual love of the outdoors and a lifelong friendship.

The camaraderie that Knowles and Moore enjoyed as children continued as the pair matured. And soon, their careers also became intertwined.

It was ironic that G. B. Knowles chose a career as an outdoor writer before Scott Moore became a guide. It was the early 1970s and there were no inshore fishing guides to speak of on the Florida gulfcoast. There were a handful of guides in the Chokoloskee region of the 10,000 Islands. But most of them were part time guides, many of them achieved their main source of income from commercial net fishing.

Sanibel Island had a few inshore guides that chartered full time for a living. But this elite area played host to wealthy tourists who saw a guided fishing trip as part and parcel of a holiday in Florida, whether they caught a lot of fish or not.

In Boca Grande tarpon fishing sustained the entire charterboat industry, but only during the summer. Boca's guides often sold insurance or practiced commercial fishing during the rest of the year.

No one fished for inshore gamesters between Tampa Bay and Crystal River. North of there a few guides dabbled with trout fishing charters between commercial fishing forays. And that was the way of inshore guiding in the gulf of Mexico during the 1970's.

In Sarasota, Captain Jonnie Walker was just getting started on what was to become a successful guiding business for trout. But

Captain Jonnie Walker of Sarasota, was one of the few fishing guides working the gulfcoast during the 1970's.

in most of the gulf of Mexico running a charterboat meant fishing offshore for grouper, snapper, king mackerel and amberjack or for tarpon during the summer.

Less than a dozen fishing guides on the west coast could claim to fish for snook with any degree of certainty. Anglers who chartered such men sometimes had outstanding days when they managed to boat a limit of snook. But those anglers were just as likely to catch nothing. Snook fishing, prior to Scott Moore's entry into the guiding business, was considered haphazard at best. To many anglers merely catching one snook was the accomplishment of a lifetime.

In those days G. B. Knowles and Scott Moore fished together for fun. Knowles was working odd jobs while trying to make it as a writer. Moore was working as a chef at a restaurant and fishing on his days off. And he spent each summer's vacation fishing for tarpon in the gulf in the morning, prowling the bays for snook in the afternoon.

Scott Moore now fishes a pair of boats, a 17-foot Shoalwater and a 24-foot Privateer with a tuna tower. But in those days Moore fished from a 15-foot Orlando Clipper he named The Primadonna. It was a name that was to be prophetic. And a name Scott continues to use -- seven vessels later.

Soon Scott Moore, and the tiny Primadonna, began regularly producing unheard of catches of snook. We aren't talking about catching four or 10 or 20 snook. Rather Moore was catching and releasing up to 100 linesiders in a day. And he broke with the west coast's snook fishing tradition in the process.

In the 1970's snook were considered meat fish. Poaching was rampant among the better hook and line fishermen. And heavy tackle, which kept the cover-loving snook from breaking off, was the order of the day. Moore broke with that tradition and began using line as light as two-pound test. And Scott continued to outfish everyone, even with the handicap of the lighter line.

All over the nation the better anglers were enjoying this light tackle revolution. And part of the reason for Scott Moore's meteoric rise as a snook guide was the use of such light lines.

Fact is, anglers enjoyed using the lighter equipment much more. It made a fishing trip a pleasure, rather than a day of grunt and groan work. And Moore's innovative use of light lines for snook accomplished one other vitally important thing.

In those days the better snook anglers, Moore included, practiced wade fishing for snook. Anglers would use the boat to catch and hold the live baits favored by snook. But the appearance of a boat hull on the clear, shallow grass flats where snook are found, would spook the fish. However, a wading sportsman presented a low profile, and that meant the angler could slip up on the snook in order to make the short casts dictated by heavier fishing lines.

When Scott Moore went to light tackle for snook it meant he could entertain the idea of chartering for snook.

For many reasons it isn't feasible for a fishing guide to ask his party to wade. Consequently, the only successful charters for snook were conducted in deep or dirty waters where the snook could not see the boat.

This was prior to today's proliferation of low profile flats boats. Without wading, most anglers thought you couldn't consistently catch snook on the flats. And you could not wade with paying customers on board.

But with long rods and very light line Scott was able to make Olympic casts to snook. And that allowed him to keep the boat away from the fish, avoid spooking them, and also keep the clients warm and dry. The rest is history. But, at that time, history was in the making.

Scott Moore with a winter snook on the first Primadonna in the 70's.

As his old buddy, I was the first writer to chronicle that history in a national magazine. I published the first story about Scott Moore's now-legendary snook fishing exploits in Saltwater Sportsman Magazine back in 1978. Subsequent stories quickly appeared in Florida Sportsman Magazine. And Scott has now been featured in hundreds of newspaper stories and dozens of magazine articles.

But in the seventies it was all brand new. And Moore's access to that kind of instant publicity helped to establish his credibility. For, in those days, most of the reading public were, frankly, skeptical of fishing guides who claimed to catch dozens and dozens of snook per trip.

Magazine stories helped lend instant credence to Moore's rising star. Meanwhile, newspaper features by Jeff Klinkenberg of the Saint Petersburg Times (Florida), Herb Allen of the Tampa Tribune, Jerry Hill of the Bradenton Herald and Byron Stout of the Fort Myers-News Press also added to his allure.

And, in a short time, Scott K. Moore was becoming the most sought after fishing guide in the nation. Today more magazine stories by writers like George Poveromo, Frank Sargeant, Jan Fogt and Boyd Pfeiffer continue to add to Moore's public image. And outdoor writers like Del Milligan of the Lakeland Ledger and Jim Hardee of the Miami Herald have spread Scott's fame around the state. But these are professional outdoor writers and they don't just make things up.

Scott Moore has enjoyed more publicity then any other fishing guide in the nation. But there is a good reason for it. He has no equal. And good writers from around the country were quick to recognize that fact.

The result of Moore's success has ironically contributed to a dwindling down of the publicity he once accrued. Scott now enjoys a stable of steady customers who charter him oneday a week or one day a month. And he is booked for years in advance during the peak snook fishing times. Hence, he isn't able to take on many new clients.

And that factor has led to a brand new industry. For as

Captain Chris Mitchell (right) is one of the younger generation of guides who has followed the snook fishing trails that Scott Moore blazed.

more and more anglers clamored for fishing trips of the type that Moore could produce the demand for fishing guides rose. Meanwhile, Moore had to turn away so many anglers that he began to send them to a new crop of fledgling guides. And, so, an inshore guiding industry grew from the overflow of anglers Scott became too busy to accommodate.

In the 18 years since the Primadonna became the first successful inshore charterboat in Tampa Bay the number of fishing guides has skyrocketed. By 1994 more than 100 guides called Tampa Bay home. Since Scott Moore began fishing in Charlotte Harbor the guide population there has also risen by twenty-fold. And the number of guides from Key West to Corpus Christie has blossomed similarly.

Consequently, the purpose of this book isn't to publicize Scott Moore, the fishing guide. Rather this volume recounts the history of the sport of modern snook fishing, and the man who single-handedly created it.

In telling that story we will also be revealing the great secrets that have made Captain Scott Moore the PRIMADONNA of fishing guides -- and a legend in the annals of sport fishing.

Chapter 2

TIGHT LIPS FOR TOMORROW

Scott Moore, like all good fishing guides, is an inveterate liar. Anything you have ever heard Moore say or anything ever written about him in the past is suspect. For no good fishermen will ever tell another the whole truth about where or how he caught fish.

Good anglers jealously guard their secrets. And there are sound reasons for this seemingly unsocial behavior -- the other guy might not be the kind of person who will treat those fish properly. Hence, good anglers share fishing secrets with others selectively. Before an angler will trust someone with a great secret he or she has to know the other angler well enough to know that such a secret will be guarded well.

Otherwise the fish -- or the guide involved -- are both liable to suffer.

If a guide finds a bunch of fish and somebody else also finds them, the guide may arrive at the spot the next day only to find another angler camped on "his" fish. If there are plenty of fish around that may not be a problem, but there aren't always plenty of fish around. So guides naturally have to guard their treasure trove of fish. They get paid to produce fish for their clients. So, to a guide, a cooperative concentration of gamefish is like finding sunken gold.

But there are worse things that can happen to a "found" concentration of fish. An unscrupulous angler called a "fish hog" could happen on them. This brand of angler may or may not be an illegal poacher. A poacher is a criminal who kills fish for profit in violation of the law. Poachers can be hook and line anglers, or commercial netters. But the fish hog

If a fish hog finds a concentration of redfish, he can wipe them out quickly.

may obey the letter of the law and still violate the spirit of the law.

One type of fish hog that is growing more and more prevalent is the type of angler who loads the boat with non-fishing people in order to be able to keep extra limits of fish. And while such practices are legal they certainly aren't ethical. There is a big difference in a guide keeping his one redfish per day limit and giving that channel bass away and someone loading the boat with people to deliberately circumvent conservation laws.

Then there is the type of fish hog who really doesn't realize what he is. He is a legal angler but not much of an ardent conservationist, he likes to keep fish. And he is going to keep the limit no matter what. If this guy finds your fish, and sits on them every day, the result is going to be the same as if an illegal poacher made one big haul.

A ban on commercial netting still won't stop all poaching.

Possession limits on many species of fish and game should prevent this behavior, but few anglers pay attention to possession limits. Most don't even know how many fish they have in their freezer, and it's even harder for the authorities to enforce such possession limits.

By the time this book makes it to print there is a good chance that inshore commercial netting in Florida will no longer exist legally. But that may not prevent renegade netters from poaching fish quietly -- at night -- the way they have for decades.

A net ban also won't stop hook and line poachers from wiping out a guide's honey hole. And it is these threats to the fish that cause guides like Scott Moore to be notoriously tight lipped about giving away the choicest of snook fishing secrets. Until now.

For things are changing on the waterfront. Today it has become trendy to favor protecting the environment. True sportsmanship is growing by leaps and bounds. And catch and release fishing is soaring in popularity. Guides like Scott Moore are largely responsible for this change in behavior.

Captain Moore was one of the first guides in the nation to voluntarily adopt catch limits on his charterboat that were

Releasing big snook like this was first popularized by Scott Moore. Such conservation practices are the keys to preserving snook for the future.

below what the law allowed. Before Moore's entry into the guiding business, gulfcoast charterboat captains measured their catch not by individual animals, but by the hundreds of pounds of fish they brought in. Self-imposed limits, like those Moore initiated, helped educate a new generation of anglers and guides, and created a movement towards voluntary conservation that is at the heart of the sport fishing industry today.

And it is Scott's belief that only such a change in behavior can effectively thwart the fish hogs and poachers.

And that is the purpose of this book. For in showing people how to catch and appreciate the snook lies the secret in saving the snook.

Saving the snook is at the heart of this book. For they are a troubled animal that may see more difficulties ahead. For Scott Moore, promoting the snook has been a way to insure for snook in the future. The nineties are no time to bury our heads in the sand and jealously guard the secrets of snook. That spirit of selflessness has colored Scott's career. It was the same spirit that led to changes in management and society that now are giving America's threatened marine resources a fighting chance.

Oddly, for the snook, management of those marine resources turned the corner at the first Snook Symposium held in Fort Lauderdale in 1983.

That landmark conference marked a new beginning for Florida's beleaguered marine resources. And the snook became the warning bell for other endangered marine animals, in Florida, and around the world.

Chapter 3

THE SNOOK SYMPOSIUMS

"Close it down," Scott Moore's voice boomed in the Fort Lauderdale meeting hall.

It shocked most of the crowd. Snook fishing guides from the east coast had just told the assembled speakers and the handful of media in the audience that snook were plentiful on the east coast and nothing needed to be done to regulate them further. Fish camp operators from Englewood pleaded that closing snook harvest during the summer would put them out of business. And, besides, they assured, there were plenty of snook.

But biologist Gerard Bruger wasn't so sure. Bruger, of the Florida Department of Natural Resources, had documented an alarming decline in the snook population of southwest Florida. This population slump had initiated the first Florida Snook Symposium -- a think tank devoted to saving the snook for the future. And it was a decline that Bruger thought could signal a devastating crash in the gulf's snook population if radical harvest limits were not imposed.

Snook are misplaced animals constantly living on the edge. These neo-tropicals are only found in the southernmost reaches of the continental U.S. And, in those locations, they are very much at the mercy of the weather.

Devastating freezes in the early sixties and the mid-70's had killed thousands of snook, resulting in alarming population declines that suggested virtual reproductive failure for several years. Such an event in an animal population can signal danger of extinction. For without a successful spawn, something biologists call recruitment, the future of the popu-

Scott Moore (right) and Mitch Rickey show off a big snook.

lation is dependent on the adults alone.

And that is a dangerous situation. It means that another freeze, or a bad red tide or some other natural disaster could kill so many adult snook that there would not be enough left to replenish the population. According to DNA research presented at the 1993 Snook Symposium such a calamity did befall the snook population in Tampa Bay at some point in the past. And it was a devastation so great that Tampa Bay's snook have still not recovered. Evidence of intense inbreeding suggests that the snook of Tampa Bay are still suffering.

But, at the time of the first snook symposium, scientists could only guess at such things. Gerry Bruger knew something was wrong with the snook population. And it seemed prudent, from Bruger's statistician point of view, to enact measures to replenish the dwindling snook population.

Those management proposals were: lowering the bag limit from four snook per day to two and closing the summer spawning months of June, July and August to harvest. Most of the fishing guides, and others concerned with snook, came to the conference to forestall such extreme measures. But Scott Moore came as an invited speaker for he had been urging new limits on the declining snook for some time. Now, as a snook guide, he was telling them to close snook fishing.

"Look, snook are in trouble," Moore told the conference.

"Two years ago I caught three thousand snook. Last year I caught less than a thousand. And there are no small snook around. I make my living off of catching snook. But I say close it down. I can fish for tarpon, or trout, or cobia during the summer. But we have to do something to help the snook. And closing snook during the summer will definitely help."

But Moore did not stop at this heresy. Instead he also urged the assembled scientists, outdoor writers and anglers to close snook fishing during the months of January and February; a time of year when cold weather puts stress on these

Mote Marine Laboratory was the site of the most recent Snook Symposium.

neo-tropical animals and a time when they are subject to easy poaching.

It was a landmark meeting. For snook, like most of Florida's saltwater resources, had received little attention from fishery managers and the politicians who fueled them. In fact, the commercial fishing industry had so controlled the legislative process in Florida that meaningful conservation of the marine fishery was practically unheard of in the first three quarters of the 20th Century.

Snook, then were the bellwether for the entire marine food chain.

These neo-tropical animals would be the first to show signs of stress related to overfishing. Snook were the first Florida fish to be removed from the list of commercial harvest when they were granted gamefish status in 1958. Before that historic day a thriving haul seine commercial fishery and a calcutta pole hook and line commercial fishery had brought snook to the brink of extinction.

Meanwhile, the highly evolved snook is one of the more sensitive of the larger marine predators to environmental factors. Their vulnerability to cold weather, pollution and loss of habitat meant the snook would be one of the early warning signs for the entire marine ecosystem. The danger to snook eggs and larvae from aerial mosquito spraying made scientists and mosquito control specialists alike take a hard look at just how harmful such practices are to all manner of marine life. And it all started with the snook symposiums.

The snook symposiums of the 1980's were the first attempt by legislators, scientists and fishery managers to sit down with every day anglers and fishing guides in order to find solutions to the problems facing marine life like the snook. Part of the reason for that was the growing romance of snook fishing created by Scott Moore and the publicity he

Snook research has allowed the next generation of youngsters to enjoy this gamefish.

generated.

Snook fishing has always been a somewhat mystical endeavor. No other saltwater fish so apes the image of the largemouth bass. And bass have become icons for the majority of American anglers. While Ernest Hemingway was writing about marlin and rainbow trout, novelists like John D. Mac Donald were romanticizing the snook.

Part of romance always is love. And Scott Moore loved the snook. They were not merely a business to him. And he fought bitterly to save them.

At Moore's insistence alone Florida did close the winter months to snook fishing. And they also went along with Bruger's advice to reduce the bag limits and close harvest during the summer. But the symposiums did much more than that. In the ensuing years additional snook meets were to be held in West Palm Beach, Sarasota and at Port of the Islands Resort near Naples. At each conference new light was shed on the problems of the snook. And, at each meeting, the interest in this odd animal grew.

During the 1993 Snook Symposium at Mote Marine Laboratory nearly 200 anglers attended the two days of sometimes highly technical talks. Brightly colored tee shirts were given to each attendee and gourmet meals were served. It was a far cry from the first symposium when a dozen fishing guides and outdoor writers constituted the entire audience. The huge increase in the popularity of the snook -- more then the symposiums -- were the keys to saving the fish.

And that popularity has translated into power at the ballot box. For snook fishermen must now purchase a saltwater fishing license and a snook stamp. That means millions of dollars in tax moneys for voters to hold politicians accountable for. And those moneys have also meant more research than ever for the curiosity that constitutes the snook.

At the first snook symposium only half a dozen scientists gave presentations on snook and most of them were mere forays into potential snook research. At that time most of the proposed research involved projects to rear snook artificially in order to replenish depleted stocks.

At the 1993 symposium it wasn't just the general public's interest in snook that had burgeoned. The scientific community also jumped on the snook bandwagon. At the Mote gathering more than 30 scientists made presentations about snook. Between the huge amount of publicity snook generated and those beckoning tax dollars, grant-hungry biologists were falling in love with *Centropomus undecimalis* along with everybody else. All it had taken was to remove the mystique from the snook that the animal had enjoyed prior to 1978.

"You see, we have showed people how to catch these snook," Scott Moore says, "because we had to."

"Back when nobody knew how to catch fish, no one would go fishing. So no one cared about the fish or the mangroves. The developers did what they wanted. Pollution was everywhere. And the poachers -- with the help of the politicians -- just raped the resource.

"The water is more crowded today. It makes it harder for a guy like me to fish. But we have limits on snook now that should help protect them for the future. We have taken steps to protect redfish, and trout and cobia. And all of those things have happened because fishing became so popular.

"It became popular because I showed people that they could go out on the water and catch fish and have a good time. Once it became popular the politicians had to listen to our concerns. So giving out secrets sometimes turns out to be a good thing."

And there are lots of secrets for prospective snook anglers to ponder.

Chapter 4

LIVING ON THE EDGE

Snook are complicated animals. And a lot of misinformation and confusion has been spread about them -- sometimes by otherwise competent anglers.

The first fallacy about snook is the odd idea that they migrate. Snook do not migrate. They move within their range the way all non-migratory fish do. But they do not migrate. Years ago some outdoor writers speculated that snook moved south during the winter and north during the summer. But such movements have more to do with expanding populations during good breeding years than any actual migration.

Along the Atlantic coast snook do move north and south quite a bit. However, these movements are merely efforts by the snook to follow moving forage fish. The classic example occurs during the famous east coast "mullet run" that happens each fall. But, even east coast snook have a home range -- and they do not migrate.

Even today some scholars speak of migrations during the winter. Yet this movement by snook is no different than a sea trout traveling from shallow grass flats to deep water channels in search of warmth. It is merely movement within a range due to environmental factors.

But snook made a great migration once, and that is the reason we enjoy this great gamefish in Florida and southern Texas today.

You see, one of the great secrets to catching snook is understanding the nature of the fish. Snook are really a misplaced animal. They simply don't belong in the continental U.S.

This 40-pound snook came from Costa Rica — the ancestral home of modern snook that call Florida and south Texas home today.

Photo, courtesy of Ed Chiles.

Today's snook are relative newcomers to the United States. During the Pleistocene epoch, 10,000 years ago, an ice age froze the oceans and dropped temperatures in the southern U.S. The continental shelf was dry land then for miles into the gulf of Mexico. Giant elephants, and wild camels roamed the land in those days. And the seas were far too cold for the tropical snook.

Florida was a different place during the Pleistocene. For instance, Tampa Bay -- today one of the largest estuaries in the world -- was probably a vast grassy plain. Flat rock can be found on the bay bottom, and this rock bears a fossil record of land animals that roamed what is now Tampa Bay during prehistory.

Similar fossiliferous rock can be found in the gulf off Venice. And, from studying these fossils, we know that estuary systems like Tampa Bay did not exist in those days. From the fossil record it appears that stingrays, drums and sharks made up the bulk of the fishes in the gulf of Mexico during the Pleistocene. In particular, the abundance of fossil teeth from the ancestor of the feared great white shark indicates just what the Pleistocene gulf may have been like. For white sharks are most common in cold water environments. And that means snook, tarpon and other tropical animals could not have lived in the gulf at that time.

But things changed. The great ice sheets melted. The waters rose and the temperatures climbed. And some adventurous snook took advantage of the warming seas to make the great migration north.

They took advantage of a period of especially warm weather -- perhaps years, perhaps centuries -- to move north, following the Mexican coast, until they reached the northern gulf.

From Texas the snook moved east, exploring the bayous of Louisiana and Mobile Bay, until they finally reached the waters of Florida's west coast.

But the snook of the late Cenozoic era weren't content to stop there. They journeyed down the coast to Florida Bay and then swam east to reach the Atlantic Ocean. So, at one point in prehistory, snook were found from the coast of northeast Florida south, and around the gulf to South America.

Perhaps ancient North American Indians fished for them along the Mississippi beaches. But they did not catch them there for long.

A cooling trend occurred and water levels fluctuated once more. And, once again, the northern gulf became too cold

Snook made a great migration thousands of years ago to reach Florida waters.

for the tropical snook. And that left the snook stranded in Florida. It also created two completely different populations of snook in the Sunshine State.

Florida Bay presented a great problem for the snook. This vast, shallow body of water is not conducive for successful reproduction of snook. Biologist Mike Tringali of the Florida Department of Natural Resources notes a strange near-absence of snook eggs and larvae in Florida Bay. And there is a good reason for that.

In order to survive, snook eggs and larvae must be able to mature in deep, open waters that are free of predators. Shallow Florida Bay simply has too many animals that eat snook eggs for a successful number of them to survive. Consequently, Florida Bay effectively creates a barrier between the snook on the east coast and those on the west coast.

Tringali has been able to use sophisticated DNA testing to determine genetic similarities between certain snook populations. The fish on the east coast more closely resemble snook in Puerto Rico and other parts of the Caribbean. Whereas the genetics of gulfcoast snook more closely resemble the snook in central and south America.

And that would seem to indicate that the populations of the two coasts have been separated for a very long time.

We don't know why the snook visited Florida with the retreat of the ice age, but they obviously found it to their liking. Yet, Florida represents the northernmost limit of the snook's range. Nature seldom does things by accident, and there had to be something in the northern gulf that would allow the neo-tropical snook to flirt with the chance of disaster that living so close to the freeze line entailed.

And there was one good reason why snook succeeded in these northern limits. Each spring and summer both coasts of Florida experience a true migration of oceanic baitfish that brings huge amounts of protein to the estuaries. This large seasonal influx of food was vital if the snook were to survive at the northern limit of its range. And understanding this unique relationship between snook and these oce-

The relationship between this small baitfish — the scaled sardine — and the snook have allowed the linesider to survive in cold water locales.

anic baitfish is one of the keys to catching this gamefish.

Perhaps that was the reason the snook made the ancient journey from their Pleistocene home. For today's oceanic baitfish are also semi-tropical animals that do not tolerate cold weather. The bait may have moved north as the waters warmed. And the snook may have followed them.

Still this ancient traveler had not forgotten its former lifestyle in Central and South American river systems. And the lost snook of Florida and south Texas adapted to the old ways.

Each fall the snook has to retreat to havens from the winter cold. Snook move up the rivers and creeks of Florida in the fall. Here they take advantage of freshwater springs and sheltered waters for protection from a killing freeze.

During the bad freeze in the 1970's three inches of snow covered the ground in Tampa, Florida, and snook died en masse at Port Manatee adjacent to the open waters of Tampa Bay. But no snook died in the upper reaches of the Manatee or Braden rivers 20 miles east of the massive kill at Port Manatee.

The high winds of a cold front produce a wind chill factor much colder than the temperature itself. Such a wind chill tends to cool open waters quickly. Yet the protected waters of the rivers and creeks does not suffer from the wind chill so. And those waters consistently stay several degrees warmer than the more open waters.

But wintering in the rivers isn't easy for the snook. There isn't a lot of food in these backwaters. And the snook's metabolism is already compromised by the cold. Cold weather snook can not afford to expend valuable energy chasing foods that they might not catch. Eventually, actively feeding becomes too risky for the snook.

Winter snook fishing has always tapered off after the first of the year. And it may mean that snook simply stop feeding completely during the depth of winter. January and February mean near-starvation for the snook. Certainly, they lose a lot of weight, for the snook that are caught in early March are often 15 pounds lighter than a comparably sized fish in July.

Such deprivation could only be tolerated if a large source of food was available for the snook when spring arrived. And the migration of schools of pilchards, threadfin herring and Spanish sardines aptly serves the plight of winter-weary snook. Snook need to put on weight quickly after the winter drought. For nature also takes advantage of the abundance of migratory baitfish by coinciding the snook's spawning season for this time of year. And reproduction puts enormous energy demands on wild animals.

Thus the snook has a unique relationship with these migratory baitfish. In fact, snook have become so dependent on these baits that using them is one of the "secrets" to catching snook.

To consistently catch snook, you must understand why one snook bait works magic where others don't. Snook are opportunists and will eat shrimp, pinfish, grunts, ballyhoo and ladyfish. But they have a special relationship with one particular type of bait.

Threadfin herring and Spanish sardines invade the estuary each spring along with massive schools of pilchards called scaled sardines (or whitebait to anglers). These three baitfish look alike and travel in schools together. Yet, if you examine them, you will find a big difference. Both the Spanish sardines and the threadfin herring are soft-bodied, soft-scaled fish that die easily.

The scaled sardine is a tough, heavily-muscled fish. Spanish sardines, threadfin herrings, shad and menhaden are strict plant eaters. They eat phytoplankton and will not feed on fish-based chum. But scaled sardines do eat fish-based chum, and they feed on zooplankton -- and that may account for their hardiness.

Consequently, scaled sardines are higher in protein then the softer-fleshed baitfish. Yet, scaled sardines are the only "hard fleshed" bait source that comes in dense enough schools to fit the energy demands of the snook. Pinfish are hard-bodied as well and probably possess as much protein. But these abundant grass flat inhabitants just don't come in the tight, vulnerable, schools that snook require in order to gain weight rapidly. For those reasons live scaled sardines make magic baits for snook.

By the time the summer rolls around snook really become targeted on whitebait, and it is often the only thing you can catch them on. Snook spawn during the summer months. And that means the linesiders congregate in large schools at this time of year. That makes for a competition factor and June and July often means the best snook fishing of the year though keeping snook is not legal during those months.

Few saltwater fish spawn as reliably as the snook. You can often catch trout with roe in them in May. But you may only find roe in one trout out of five. With snook it's different. Between May and August all of the snook you catch will have roe.

The winter adaptation of the snook, and its special relationship with the scaled sardine, are just a couple of the snook's survival techniques. Nature employs another tool for snook during the spawn.

Snook are hermaphroditic. Biologist Ron Taylor of the Florida Marine Research Institute (FDNR) found indisputable evidence of sex reversal in snook after researchers speculated about it for years. Snook begin life as males and turn into females as they grow larger. Such hermaphroditism may play a role in the snook's advanced survival skills. And it may have to do with courtship displays.

Like many freshwater fish, snook appear to engage in courtship displays. Large snook, which are invariably females, will often "stand on their heads," floating nose down with the tips of their tails sticking out of the water. These fish are not feeding, like a tailing bonefish would be. And such

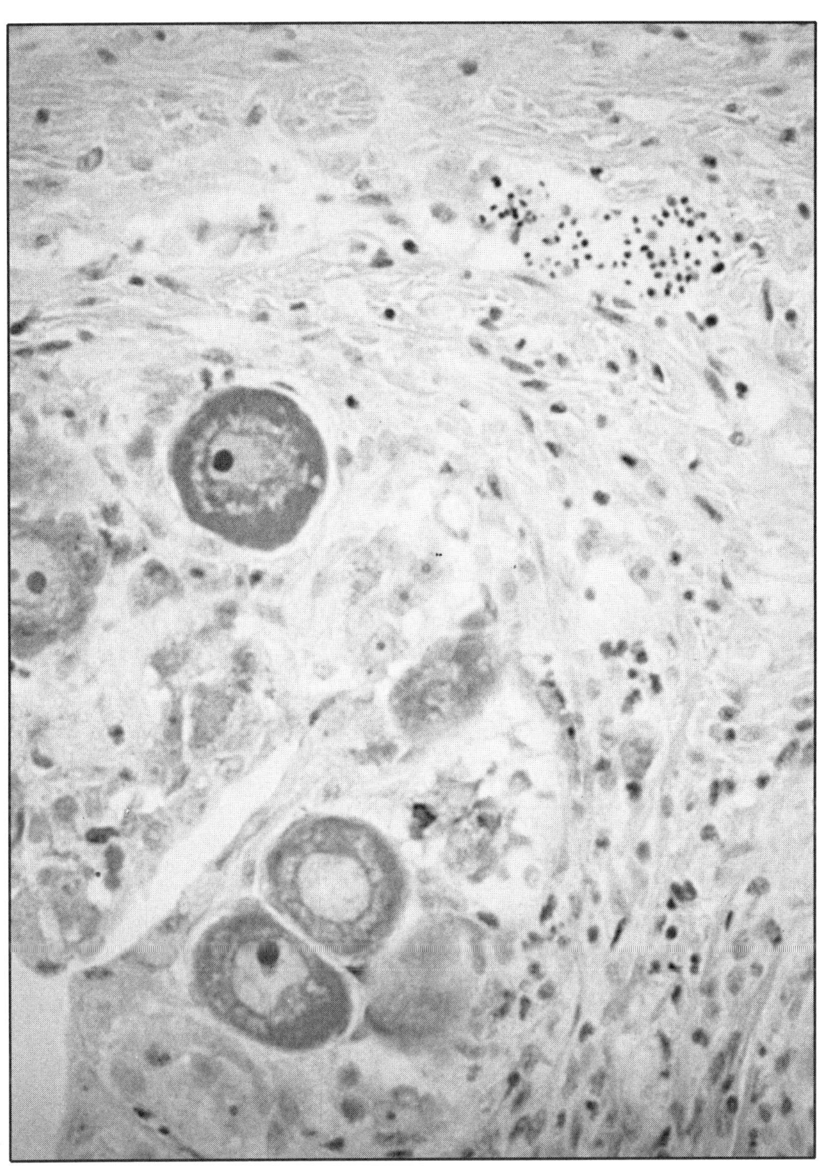

This microscopic photograph of a snook's reproductive system demonstrates how these intricate animals are able to change sex. In the photograph the smaller black dots are the sperm of the original male snook. The larger round items are developing female eggs as the fish begins to change from male to female as it grows larger. Photo courtesy of Ron Taylor.

"tailing" females are often being circled by smaller males.

Such a courtship display may serve to attract males to a gravid female so that spawning will be more successful. Meanwhile, the snook has made one adaptation during the spawn that has greatly aided the fish's survival.

Snook spawn in or near passes and inlets during the full and new moons during the summer. Snook spawn in the late afternoon and night during those times. And the full and new moons are important. These lunar phases not only produce strong tides. But the tide is always falling during summer afternoons when the moons are full or new. And that's important to the snook.

The worst place for snook eggs and larvae to be is over the shallow grass flats and around mangroves. This is great habitat for adult snook. But snook eggs and larvae would quickly be gobbled up by the abundant pinfish and other denizens of these inshore areas.

The falling afternoon tides of the big summer moons allows snook eggs and larvae to mature in the open waters where such predators are scarce.

Extreme sensitivity to changes in temperature, a unique relationship with one particular food source and highly evolved reproductive behavior all make the snook an unusual animal. And understanding these things about the fish can help you catch more of them.

Snook, perhaps more then any other fish, do things for a reason.

Scott Moore has pinpointed a number of reasons why snook do certain things. One of them is called "the incoming tide blues."

In the spring snook often will not feed while the tide is coming in. But, with no change in water depth, they will begin to feed when the tide starts out.

Lots of anglers know this. And most of them assume the falling tide sweeps food from the mangroves and grass flats to the waiting snook; in effect, providing chum for them.

But Scott, correctly, disputes that theory.

"The incoming tide brings water up from the depths to the shallows," Moore explains.

"This water is cooler than the shallower water over the flat. And this cooler water lowers the snook's metabolism. But, after that water has been on the flat during a four-hour tidal stage, it is warmed by the sun. Consequently, the snook's metabolism goes up as the water warms. And by the time the tide starts moving again the snook are ready to feed."

Most fish are more tolerant of subtle changes in temperature. But, for the snook, drops in the mercury can be life-threatening.

Life in the United States truly is "living on the edge" for *Centropomus undecimalis* and his kin.

Chapter 5

CATCHING AND USING LIVE BAIT

In chapter four we explained the intricate evolutionary pattern that has resulted in a special relationship between snook and one particular prey species in the United States. Snook -- depending on where they are found -- may eat many things. But to entertain the idea of catching them consistently you must be able to offer them the baits that their life cycle is so closely tied to.

That fish is known to scientists as the scaled sardine. It's scientific name is *Harengula jaguana*. Snook anglers call them whitebait, pilchards, shiners and greenbacks. Scott calls them crickets. In the Florida Keys the guides call them worms. They go by such nicknames because they represent as sure a bite for most saltwater fish as worms and crickets do on the farm pond.

But you can seldom buy this magic bait. And, if you want to catch snook consistently, you will needs lots of them. Hence, it will be necessary for the snook angler to catch and house his own in a baitwell. And catching the whitebait in quantities necessary for successful snooking is often the hardest part of the day.

The schools of scaled sardines over-winter in the Florida Keys and make their way north along both Florida coasts during the spring. If the weather is warm these pilchards can be found as early as January. In fact, during warm winters some schools of whitebait never leave their summer haunts.

The whitebait of March first -- the opening day of snook season -- are often very hard to catch. Like snook these, tropical baitfish aren't active in cooler seas and that makes them harder to catch. One trick to catching this early bait is to find them before the sun comes up around lights that fall on the water.

In order to catch whitebait it's helpful if you are able to concentrate them in thick schools before you throw a bait castnet over the mass of small fish. To accomplish this task chum is used to provide free food for the pilchards and concentrate them in a feeding frenzy.

One reason early scaled sardines are hard to catch is because they don't chum well. Part of the reason for that is the lowered metabolism that the cooler water means to the whitebait. Perhaps the reason early bait is found at night around light is because marine zooplankton like copepods are attracted to light. Pilchards feed on these microscopic relatives of shrimp and crabs. So a light source over water provides a natural chum slick. And that means the shiners don't have to expend too much energy to catch food around night lights.

Whether you have to get bait around the lights or after sunup the chum is becoming more and more important. In the 1970's a couple of cans of Kozy Kitten catfood and a loaf of old bread was all the chum a snook angler needed. But with the massive growth in snook fishing the bait, along with the snook, have become educated.

Pilchards in the nineties behave much differently than they did in the seventies. They are much spookier and less likely to chum. So some sophisticated chum recipes have been developed.

Scott uses a mix that is part his recipe, part that of Captain Larry Mendez and partly the work of Captain Jim O'Neill. He likes to use stone ground grain bread, a Mendez contribution, and corn meal or grits, ala O'Neill. This mixture, rather than plain old bread, gives a fluffy texture to the chum.

But the grain products only help suspend the chum in the

water column long enough for the whitebait to find it. Pilchards are carnivores that eat larvae and zooplankton, so you have to add a fish or shrimp product to the grain for flavor.

Kozy Kitten still works reasonably well. Meanwhile, Alpo's Salmon and Shrimp Treat catfood is also excellent chum. Lots of anglers use canned Jack Mackerel. But Scott swears by canned sardines -- the cheapest you can buy. Not the fancy hors d'oeuvres smothered in mustard sauce.

He also likes to add oil to whitebait chum. Store-bought menhaden oil works very well, but is also quite expensive. But mere cooking oil also helps. Scott maintains that oil added to chum helps slick the surface of the water and allows the bait to find the chum.

Anise oil added to chum also improves the mixture. In fact, some baitfish, notably ballyhoo, will not chum well unless anise is added to the chum.

Using your own castnet is the only way to get good snook bait.

For a bait net Moore likes 22 pounds of lead for a fast sinking net in deep water. Whitebait is often found around offshore wrecks, over artificial reefs or around large range and channel markers. So the extra lead can be a help if you have to catch bait in deep water.

Scott recommends large handfuls of chum lumped deep in deep water or when the bait stays deep. But that is exactly the wrong way to chum in most scenarios. And the vast majority of anglers -- including some very good guides -- don't understand the mechanics of chumming for bait -- or snook.

Chumming for bait if often the hardest part of the day.

Tiny pinches of chum ladled in a steady stream is the way to ball up whitebait in most shallow water situations. This steady dribble takes a bit of patience, but once the bait is ganged up it's easier to catch. One curious thing about finicky bait is the fact that it often chums better after the net has been thrown over it a couple of times; the action of hauling the net in over the grass flat stirs up plankton that is hidden in the grass thus creating a natural chum slick.

Bait is a lot easier to catch on grass flats during the incoming tide. The rising tide washes zooplankton onto the flat and that produces natural food for the bait.

A good guide often has to catch bait several times a day. No baitwell is large enough (on inshore boats) to hold as much whitebait as a hot day of snook fishing demands. And if you have to catch bait in the midst of catching snook that may mean finding it far from where you caught the first batch in the morning. And that means keeping an eye open for bait when you don't know where it is.

Diving birds can lead you to bait schools. And the way they behave can indicate just exactly what type of bait they are after.

"The Royal tern will show you where the whitebait is," Scott notes.

"But so will the pelican if you know what to look for."

Pelicans alter their dives depending on the type of bait they are after. Quick, turning, shallow dives by pelicans who then hold their heads under the water almost always mean glass minnows are the target. Sea gulls sitting on the pelicans head after a dive also indicates these tiny, unusable baitfish.

Meanwhile, long high dives by pelicans usually mean shad (menhaden), Spanish sardines and threadfin herring are the target. Don't bother with these baits. They are plant eaters that will not chum. And they are soft, delicate baits that die easily. Snook will eat them. But they don't make good baits.

Short, straight dives by pelicans are the thing to look for if you want whitebait. That and piping, dipping terns.

Don't be tempted by scaled sardines look-a-likes in the quest for bait. Spanish sardines and threadfin herring often travel with pilchards. But they don't make good baits. All three of these migratory baitfish feature shimmery silver sides. But you can distinguish between them easily. The Spanish sardine is more elongated then the threadfin or the whitebait. Meanwhile, threadfins have tiny string-like trailer fins that project from the dorsal fin, much like a tarpon.

Threadfin herring also have spots on them while scaled

Pelicans eat the same bait that snook do, and can help in finding that bait.

sardines don't. But the best way to tell these fish apart is to handle them. Spanish sardines and threadfin herring are soft, delicate animals. And their scales come off easily when handled. Scaled sardines are hardy and you just about have to use a fish scaler to take the scales off of them. That hardiness is one of the things that makes them such good baits.

Other baits also have their place in snook fishing. Often big snook will only eat unusual things. Live grunts are good for lunkers and are best caught with pinfish hooks over eel grass beds adjacent to hard white sand. Squid rather than cut shrimp is the best bait for grunts. If you are in a hurry and the grunts are thick you can chum with squid and use the cast net. Or you can buy grunts in many bait shops.

Pinfish are so plentiful that you will usually catch all of those you need while netting whitebait. But pinfish may be the poorest snook bait of all.

During the early 1970's one of the few snook guiding operations in the country, prior to Scott Moore, occurred in Redfish Pass off Captiva Island. And a number of outdoor writers touted the magic of pinfish for the big linesiders of that region. Neither Scott or I could understand why pinfish worked so well for snook there, and so poorly for snook in other areas.

After trying pinfish for snook in Redfish Pass I still didn't know what the guides there were doing right. I couldn't catch one on a pinfish.

Finally, one of the guides confessed. What they were calling pinfish was in fact a look-a-like -- the grunt. If you live on the east coast you will know it as the pigfish, and you will understand the deception.

Sugar trout like this one and other unusual baits will often tempt finicky snook when whitebait won't.

Like pinfish, plenty of Spanish sardines, threadfin herrings and cigar minnows (round scad) will also be accidentally netted along with the pilchards. And these can be reserved for large, finicky snook.

But two magic snook baits require some extraordinary preparations. Ballyhoo are deadly for big snook, and they are found on grass flats along with scaled sardines. Yet 'hoos are shy and hard to chum. Put that anise oil in the chum and ballyhoo tame right down and are easily netted.

Mutton minnows are another deadly bait for big snook. But they aren't found on the grass flats or around deepwater structure that holds pilchards. Instead these small mojarras are netted over hard white sand in and near passes. Mutton minnows are also thick up the rivers in the winter. And they can be caught here with blind throws of the net over sand bars. However, most winter sand perch (mojarra) have grown up and are way too big for use as a snook bait.

And you can always buy jumbo shrimp for the extra picky snook.

Still whitebait will be the standby. And there are many tricks to fishing these snook staples.

Probably the most misunderstood thing about snook fishing is live chumming with scaled sardines. Snook can be very effectively chummed with such baits but there are right times and wrong times to chum. And there are good and bad ways to do it.

Snook are chummed with crippled shiners for a number of reasons. Most linesider anglers believe that chumming is done to excite the snook into biting. Yet this is only one application of chumming.

"It's stupid to chum first before fishing," Scott says.

"If the fish are locked in and ready to bite then all chumming does is allow the tide to carry the chummed baits away. And those hungry snook that were going to bite anyway follow the chum off and away from the ones with hooks in them."

This is especially true during the fast tides of the new and full moon. Or when a south or west wind affects a quarter moon tide and speeds it up.

Scott chums as much to hold snook in an area as to turn them on into biting.

"You often don't know which way the snook are going to go when they move down, or off a flat. By chumming you can keep them with you longer, and when you watch them pop a bait, you can tell which way they are going. And that means you can follow them out, and that means catching a lot more of them while THE BITE is going on."

Snook, like most fish, tend to bite all at once. And being there on the bite and getting baits into the water then, is one of the keys to catching lots of snook.

Overchumming not only spreads out "locked in" snook that were going to bite anyway, but it can also fill them up. And, as snook become more and more educated the wisdom of offering them free, hookless, baits becomes more clouded.

In the late 1980's Scott adapted counter methods to avoid overchumming. He likes to cast four baits into a snook lair. And the presence of multiple hooked baits in close proximity to the snook achieves much the same result as chumming.

Another flaw with overchumming is the sea birds this activity attracts. Sea gulls, pelicans, terns and cormorants all come to crippled chum. And they can spoil a day of fishing. So some sneaky techniques must be employed if chumming is the order of the day and the birds are bad.

Pilchards that are hooked in the belly come off the hook easily. So Scott often casts a belly-hooked bait into a snook hole then jerks hard on the line to yank the bait off. This action puts pilchards into the water without telegraphing the action to the birds -- or other anglers.

Whitebait can also be tossed up under the mangroves if the birds are bad.

In order to chum effectively, three or four pilchards should be taken from the bait tank and hand squeezed. Squeezing them stuns them for a moment and tends to make them swim around drunkenly. Snook are predators and their role in nature is to remove the sick, weak and otherwise genetically inferior animals from the gene pool. This strengthens the gene pool of the scaled sardine and ensures the survival of the species.

So it is the nature of the snook, as a predator, to attack what it perceives to be an injured baitfish. And that accounts for the effectiveness of chumming with whitebait.

But the snook has to be in the right frame of mind, even to react to crippled pilchards. So, good times to chum are often when you are expecting a bite to be forthcoming. That might mean a tide change or an upcoming Solunar Period. Or it might be because it's getting late and everything else has failed.

The best times to chum are on the slow quarter moon tides because the chum will stay in the area rather than be swept downtide by the racing current of the big moons.

Chumming can also be done to locate snook when you don't know exactly where they are. In the 90's, with hundreds of anglers out there on the snook flats, the last thing a guide wants to do is to run the motor while looking for snook. By chumming on a flat and watching where a snook blasts a bait out of the water you can locate snook without spooking them.

On the flats whitebait is generally hooked through the hard, clear cartilage in the nose. Spanish sardines and threadfin herring are hooked the same way. Creek chubs and mutton minnows are hooked from the bottom lip up through the upper lip. A ballyhoo doesn't have an upper lip, so it is simply hooked at the base of the bottom bill.

Pinfish and grunts are hooked in the back, under the dorsal fins. However, grunts are often hooked further towards the tail than pinfish. Both of these baits are husky critters and will burrow in the grass unless a popping cork is used, or they are fished in deep water or over sand.

Popping corks will sometimes work on snook -- especially big snook -- when nothing else will. However, snook throw off cork rigs rather easily when they jump.

Standard terminal gear for live bait fishing includes 10 feet of doubled line, 18-inches of 30 to 50-pound clear monofilament and a 2/0 hook. If the bait is small, or the fish are spooky, smaller hooks might have to be used.

Live bait can provide lots of snook action like this!

For many reasons, understanding the use of bait, in snook fishing, is the most important facet of the sport. Few inshore gamefish rely so heavily on baitfish migrations as does the neo-tropical snook.

That's the main reason for the revolution that has created modern snook fishing. For when the scaled sardine and the snook come together -- in their intricate dance -- live bait is the only way to catch this gamefish.

Chapter 6

FISHING THE FLATS

Before 1978 snook were not thought of as flats fishing targets. To most anglers in the 1970's flats fishing meant visiting the Florida Keys or the Caribbean in pursuit of bonefish, permit or tarpon. Snook were considered inhabitants of mangrove creeks, piers or rivers. Clear, skinny water and snook just did not go together.

We know better now. For the west coast of Florida now rivals the Keys in flats fishing for tarpon. And flats fishing for snook is the fastest growing sport in the nation.

The truth is that all gamefish use shallow grass flats. And the key to catching them is that word "use." Everything from 1,000-pound sharks to grouper visit the grass flats. But no gamefish, including the snook, live there.

In order to fish the flats successfully you have to know why fish go there. And you have to know what problems visiting the flats entail for them.

Turtle and eel grass and other types of marine vegetation require enormous amounts of sunlight to thrive. Consequently, marine grasses can only grow in shallow water. Suspended sediment in deeper water prevents sunlight from penetrating to the bottom where sea grasses grow.

So grass flats occur on the shallow sloping waters adjacent to shorelines. Something else thrives on the shore itself.

In warm seas the mangrove is the staff of life for the marine environment. Mangroves serve many functions. They prevent shoreline erosion. They offer shelter to juvenile snook, redfish, trout and other gamefish. And they are the first link in the marine food chain.

Mangrove leaves fall into the waters of the near shore grass flats and begin to decompose. This substance, called detritus, provides food for microscopic algae. This algae provides food for microscopic animals called zooplankton. And the zooplankton means food for small pinfish, killifish (also called snook or creek chubs) and that magic snook bait called scaled sardines.

Meanwhile, plant eaters like mullet and glass minnows (another favorite snook food) graze on the algae that grows on the mangrove detritus.

So this mangrove eatery lures the food that snook eat to the flats. Meanwhile, the grass itself provides cover for that forage. And that is why snook visit the flats -- to eat.

And that's why flats fishing is so effective. For many cases you will be fishing for snook that Scott Moore calls "locked in" fish.

Locked in snook are fish that have found a place where they know food will become available. They are hungry and

Grass flats adjacent to mangroves are the places to find snook.

waiting for the food to come within range. These are not traveling fish that are looking for food. Locked in snook know that they are in the right place to encounter food. And they will stay in that spot to feed, sometimes, regardless of the pressure put on them.

But, like bonefish, snook usually don't like to venture into skinny water unless the tide is high. It isn't because they don't like shallow water. On some grass flats the very best snook fishing occurs when the tide is low. But these flats are usually large areas with deep pockets, and the vastness of such flats provides something that is important to the tidal ventures of most snook.

Snook move into shallow water during the higher tidal stages for one simple reason. Zooplankton is moved onto the flat by a rising tide. Pilchards and other snook foods follow the zooplankton onto the flat. And the snook follow their prey. The same thing happens with wildebeest migrations and lions in Africa, but with snook and plankton it happens about every 12 hours. Remember snook starve during the winter. They must put on weight rapidly while the food is available. They feed as often and as round the clock as they can.

Of course, once the zooplankton finds the easy food source in the mangrove detritus it breeds. And that makes more food for pilchards. More dinners for snook.

Usually snook leave the flats as the tide falls. But it depends on the flat. At Sister Key, in Sarasota Bay, there are some truly enormous deepwater basins situated on the flats. Similar deep holes can be found at Bull Bay in Charlotte Harbor and all around Sanibel and Captiva Island.

Such depressions are called potholes. And they may range from the gigantic "Swimming Hole" at Sister Key -- an acre-wide monster -- to a pothole the size of a Volkswagen. These potholes are geographic oddities. They are actually ancient sinkholes caused by freshwater settling and eroding

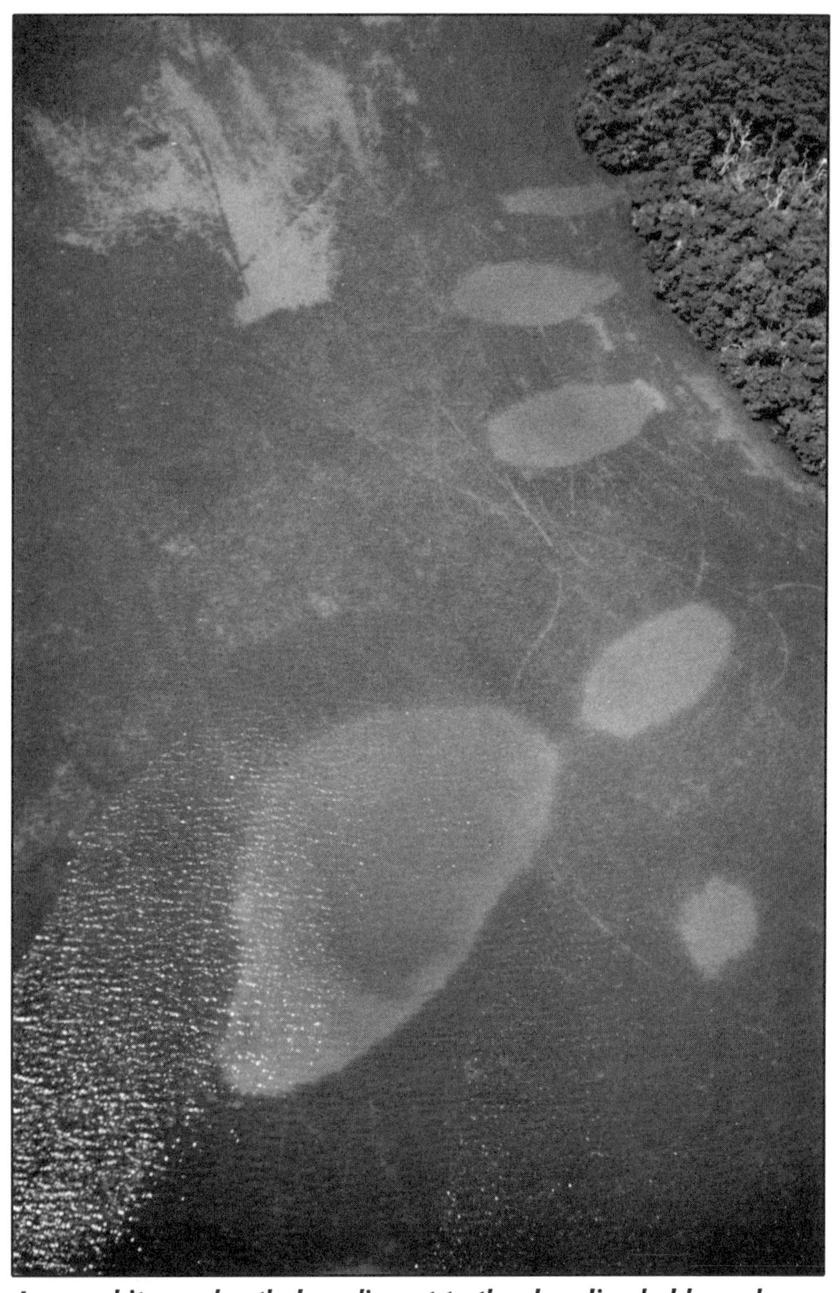

Large white sand potholes adjacent to the shoreline hold snook during high tide. *Photo by Jack Elka.*

the underlying limestone formation that is the beginning of the Florida aquifer.

During the Pleistocene, when most southern estuaries were dry land, freshwater runoffs created depressions in the underlying limestone. We still have it on dry land, but you often don't see it because of the underbrush. But, once water covered these depressions and created coastal bays, these ancient hollows really stood out.

In the northern gulf such potholes may appear as mere dimples on the bottom. But Florida's waters are younger geologically then the northern gulf. Consequently, potholes on the flats of Florida are quite prominent features.

Because these areas are deeper than the surrounding grass flat, marine grasses do not grow in them. Hence, potholes

Bottlenose dolphin (porpoise) like these are the most dangerous non-human snook predator. These intelligent, high speed marine mammals can ruin snook fishing and will go far out of their way to eat a linesider — even chasing them into shallow water.

are easily spotted as bright, white sand holes on an otherwise dark turtle grass backdrop.

On the large deeper flats, like those at Sister Key, enormous potholes can be found. These huge basins are often 10 feet deep. And they tend to hold plankton and keep the outgoing tide from sweeping it from the flat. In such locations snook food often stays on the flat throughout the tidal phases.

Meanwhile, big deep potholes make snook feel more at home.

Grass flats and mangroves are not safe places to be. I once saw a bottlenose dolphin flush a snook off a mangrove point and chase it into water so shallow that the mammal's body was out of the water. The porpoise caught the snook in water less than 18 inches deep and half-beached itself in the process. It took a considerable amount of flapping around before the porpoise half-rolled to deeper water. And it would have never made it if it had not been in the soft marl bottom of the 10,000 Islands.

Snook like this are found in white sand areas on grass flats during high tide.

These marine mammals are the number one predator of the snook. Most sharks, tarpon and other large predators simply can't catch the elusive snook. But porpoise are death on line-siders. And a snook on a shallow grass flat is like a candy store to a group of bottlenose dolphins.

Brian Shaffer is pleased with this flats snook.
Photo by Patti Knowles.

And, while sharks can't catch most snook they do take their toll. I had a snook bitten in half by a small shark after being released on another 10,000 Islands flat. Scott has watched similar carnage on the flats.

In Boca Grande the abundant ospreys eat small snook -- easy pickings for the fish hawk on a shallow grass flat. But it isn't just the porpoise or the ospreys the linesider has to worry about. People are the biggest problem for flats snook.

Scott caught one snook that had a healed over wound where an eye had once been. A spear had caused the injury.

Yet, the snook, a healthy 16-pounder, was doing just fine. Meanwhile, the increased boat traffic on the flats terrorizes the snook. They feel safer in the deep potholes on the big flats. Hence, they will stay there even during the falling tide.

If you can find them in such a location you can sometimes really nail them. If they get stuck in a deep pothole on a shallow flat, then they are usually stuck till high water returns. And they sometimes get stuck in a hole that doesn't have any bait in it. If that's the case you have a scenario for a mighty hungry snook.

If you can pole a boat quietly to these low water flats fish it's often a chance at some terrific fishing. Big flats, deep potholes and low tide often mean locked in snook. And when it does, look out.

But the majority of flats fishing involves poling the boat to the mangroves on high water and fishing deep pockets there. Potholes provide deep pockets. But there are other areas to fish.

Nearly all mangrove shorelines have a deeper sand channel that runs along the shore between the bushes and the grass flat. Snook can often be found here at high water. But catching them this close to the mangroves is another story. For snook are famous for racing to the bushes once they are hooked.

Sometimes snook can be found on the grass itself, in a somewhat deeper part of the flat. In fact, the growing popularity of snook fishing and many of the misconceptions that go along with it, have changed the behavior of modern snook. They don't lock in to the potholes the way they once did. And you often find them over grass more than you used to.

Ignorant anglers have so harried the snook that they tend to stay in the grass more these days. So if you fish the flats learn to use a push pole. Motoring over a flat looking for snook is fine if you are sight seeing. But poling is a much

As the tide begins to fall, snook drop away from the potholes next to the mangroves and begin to move off the grass flats to the channel edge. However, they often follow the potholes further out on the flat in the process. By following the fish from the near-shore holes to those closer to the channel, the angler can continue to fish the snook as they are forced to move by the outgoing water. *Photo by Jack Elka.*

better method of looking for snook, and fishing them.

Whether you use live bait, such as pilchards, or lures, flats fishing is pretty much the same. It's important to approach a pothole or a deep mottled bottom quietly.

"The worst thing you can do is bang on the hull of the boat," Scott says.

"And flats fish can really see out of the water. I chummed up a bunch of ladyfish once and hooked one and dragged it back and forth three feet off the water. And I watched that ladyfish follow that bait, watching it, out of the water.

"When you are fishing the flats you need to wear green, gray or blue shirts, pants and hats. It just drives me crazy when I have guys show up in the morning for a fishing trip with a white shirt or hat on. That's why my boat is painted green and gray."

Staying off the fish is important too. If you think you can just barely make a cast to the spot you want to fish, then you are probably a bit too close.

Many lures are hard to use on the flats because of the abundant floating grass pulled up by manatees, boat propellers and shrimp nets. Sometimes a surface lure is out of the question, but jigs and spoons work okay when the grass is heavy, especially if you toss them into potholes with clear sand bottoms. Weedless flies are also an effective tool on the flats.

But snook don't mind if a live and frisky whitebait is covered by a bit of grass. And they don't mind a grass-draped grunt either. Part of the secret of flats fishing for snook is using live bait because of the floating grass alone.

As the tide drops out most flats snook retreat with it. And that means following them out. High water snook may loll in potholes scant inches from the mangroves, but as the tide falls those snook will ease off the flat, usually following the deeper trails.

Snook are like deer. They have certain trails they like to use, if they aren't disturbed. Certain areas of a flat may be deeper than others and the early fish will follow these trails on their way off the flat during the falling tide.

These deeper parts of the flats often feature deeper potholes and swash channels that snook use as they move. Consequently, you can follow the fish off the flat, catching them as they go. But, once again, you must use the push pole or wade. Motoring on a flat with the tide falling might work great for a day or two. But in the long run it's a recipe for snook fishing failure.

When the grass starts to blossom on the top of the water and the wading birds gather the tide is about done. And that is usually the end of flats fishing till the next rising tide.

But it isn't the end of the snook's feeding foray. Only part of his career is spent on the flats. A good angler has to be able to catch him regardless of how the tide or lunar phase dictates his position.

Chapter 7

CATCHING SNOOK IN DEEP WATER

Fishing for snook in deepwater offers different challenges then fishing for snook on the flats. And there are many reasons for fishing deepwater snook.

The most obvious reason for fishing for snook in deep water is the lower tidal stages. During low water most snook will abandon the shallow grass flats they use at high tide. And that may force the angler to fish for snook in the depths.

Dropping tides on the skinniest flats means snook must leave the shallows. And, depending on the moon and the wind, that departure can be rapid. During the full and new moons the tide can drop fast once it starts out. And that drop can become even quicker if a north wind blows, for north winds cause the tide to go lower than normal. North winds and new moons can mean that the snook will hightail it off a flat the moment the tide turns. And those conditions mean little tide for flats fishing. So you must fish in deep water.

Even if a south or west wind holds the tide up for awhile, the snook will eventually leave most shallow grass flats. You can sometimes follow them out, fishing as you go. But a better plan sometimes involves ambush.

Snook will follow the deep sand, potholes and swash channels; finally ending up on the edge of the flat -- often a quarter of a mile from the mangroves they patrolled just hours earlier. It's the same thing with bonefish and permit in the Florida Keys. Only snook are schooling fish that will hang

Snook are found in deep water as well as on the shallow grass flats.

in certain areas. And that makes them much easier to fish during the falling tide.

Outer bars and flat edges are just a couple of deep water snooking prospects during the lower stages of the tide. But deep water can also be found near or on a flat itself. In the previous chapter we talked about the massive deepwater potholes of Sister Key and why snook often remain in such areas even during the lowest of tides.

But shallow flats often lead into basins that eventually lead to the edge of the flat. And snook will sometimes hole up in these areas as well. Low water snook on flat edges, or those holed up in basins, are often good targets for artificial lures because such deeper waters are often dirtier than the clear incoming tidal waters of the shallow grass flats. But the last of the outgoing tide also means lots of floating grass. So lure fishermen are better off with deep running artificials that get beneath the grass.

Snook will often drop off points and passes during the

falling tide. But low water isn't the only time to fish for linesiders in such deep water areas. The slower quarter moon tides are tailor-made for fishing off points and in passes. During the slower tides of the quarter moons there is a lot more movement of water around such areas. Hence, the fish usually are more interested in biting here.

And that current exchange means a steadier supply of bait than a flat possesses during the weaker lunar phases. So quarter moons often see snook staying in deep water regardless of the tide.

Classic cases of this occur off Rattlesnake Key in Terra Ceia Bay, Port Manatee in Tampa Bay and in Stump Pass off Englewood.

True pass fishing happens further south at Sanibel and Captiva Islands. Meanwhile, the 10,000 Islands river mouths also feature good pass fishing for snook as do the many deep inlets along the Atlantic Ocean.

Deep basins adjacent to shallow grass flats are good spots to find fish at low tide. *Photo by Jack Elka.*

Oyster bars are another choice for deepwater fishing. The current that swings around oyster bars hollows out deep holes around the bar. And this gives snook a deepwater refuge in the midst of a flat, with lots of water moving around it. Oyster bars are also good choices for fishing the slower tides.

There is a lot of controversy over how to find snook. Twenty five years ago snook fishermen frequently looked for snook from running boats over the grass flats. But there are a lot more snook anglers now. And the fish have become quite educated. So looking for snook with the boat engine running is a poor way to fish a flat today.

Yet, snook in deep water can be found with the engine running. Deep water snook are tolerant of boat engines, where motors over shallow grass flats are unnatural things to snook. So, you can find snook in deeper water with the boat

Catching snook on live bait in deep water may require changes in techniques. For instance, live pilchards often need to be hooked in the belly rather than the nose. In this photo Scott Moore's thumb indicates the correct hook placement for belly-hooking bait.

engine running. Ski Alley at Stump Pass is loaded with snook and water skiers. They coexist for one reason; this is deep water and the snook just don't feel threatened there.

One of the best places to fish for snook in deep water is along the beaches of the gulf of Mexico and the Atlantic Ocean.

Fishing deeper waters often means changes in technique as well. Most snook are taken with a simple monofilament leader of 30 to 50-pound test line. The leader is tied directly to the line with a line to leader connection like the improved blood knot, Albright Special or Uni-Knot. A 2/0 hook completes the rig if you are using live bait. Otherwise the leader is attached to your favorite artificial lure.

But in the deeper water you may find the fish won't rise to take a surface bait like fish will on the flats. Meanwhile, deep water usually means more current, and that can drag the bait and make it look unnatural.

In those situations a small rubbercore sinker can help hold a bait down. If the sinker is used the bait should be hooked in the nose so it trails naturally behind the weight.

Most baitfish will swim down if they are hooked in the belly. But a belly-hooked bait will be pulled unnaturally by the tide. So using belly-hooked bait in deep water areas may mean utilizing a controlled drift, much the way tarpon are fished in Boca Grande Pass.

Sea anchors and electric trolling motors can both be used to control a snook drift. This method of fishing works especially well in big passes. However, it can also be very valuable in places like Port Manatee where bait placement is often critical.

Scott doesn't believe much in fishing for snook around docks. Yet these deepwater areas offer some terrific snook fishing particularly at night and during the slower tides.

In the early spring and fall, canals also afford good deepwater snooking. During late spring and early fall, snook will be thick along the beaches. And while you will often find them in inches of water here, the snook along the gulf beach should be considered deep water fish.

Snook can be found in many areas along the gulf beaches. But structure plays a role in beach snooking as well as in the backwaters. Beach snook are found around downed trees, storm-ruined houses and rock piles. The March storm of 1993 washed one old house into the gulf on Palm Island near Boca Grande. It turned into a top spot for snook, as are any number of Australian Pines that have been washed into the gulf along the west coast.

In 1992 Hurricane Andrew wreaked havoc along the Atlantic shore, but, in the process the storm also provided additional habitat for beach snook there. East coast snook often follow schools of migrating mullet some distance offshore, harrying this baitfish along the way. But, even during the mullet run, those snook eventually have to return to the surf line, and any structure that a storm may have deposited there.

Deep water snook can often be finicky eaters due to the opportunism they enjoy. A flats snook has to eat during the tidal stage. He goes onto the flat to get food. But snook in passes and off points can get picky.

The Manatee River side of Emerson Point provides such a case in point. These fish see so many different kinds of baits swept past them that they have become famous for their finicky eating habits. One day they will eat live pilchards, with shrimp on the list the next. One day they will prefer mutton minnows, while grunts are the piece de resistance at other times.

Catching snook in deep water means understanding this opportunism. In short, while you are snooking in deepwater it won't hurt to have several different kinds of bait to offer.

Scott saw the greatest example of opportunism by deep water snook one summer day in 1990.

"I was running along the beach off Manasota Key looking for tarpon when suddenly I saw herds of snook swimming around like crazy with their backs out of the water," Moore says.

"I couldn't figure out what they were doing, until I looked over the side and began seeing baby loggerhead turtles."

A sea turtle nest had hatched during the night and the snook had happened on the baby turtles. And snook, like sea birds and raccoons, are predators that are not adverse to dining on young turtles.

Now we don't recommend that you use baby turtles for snook bait. It is highly illegal. But some day, some smart lure manufacturer might begin marketing turtle look-a-likes for use on snook. After all they make mouse imitations for large-mouth bass and muskelunge!

And, like bass, deepwater snook have the option of taking advantage of many different food sources.

Fishing for them in these regions often means switching tactics from the tried and true methods on the flats.

Deep water snook present different scenarios of fishing. For while flats snook are often dependent on weather and moon phase and temperature, linesiders in deep water are

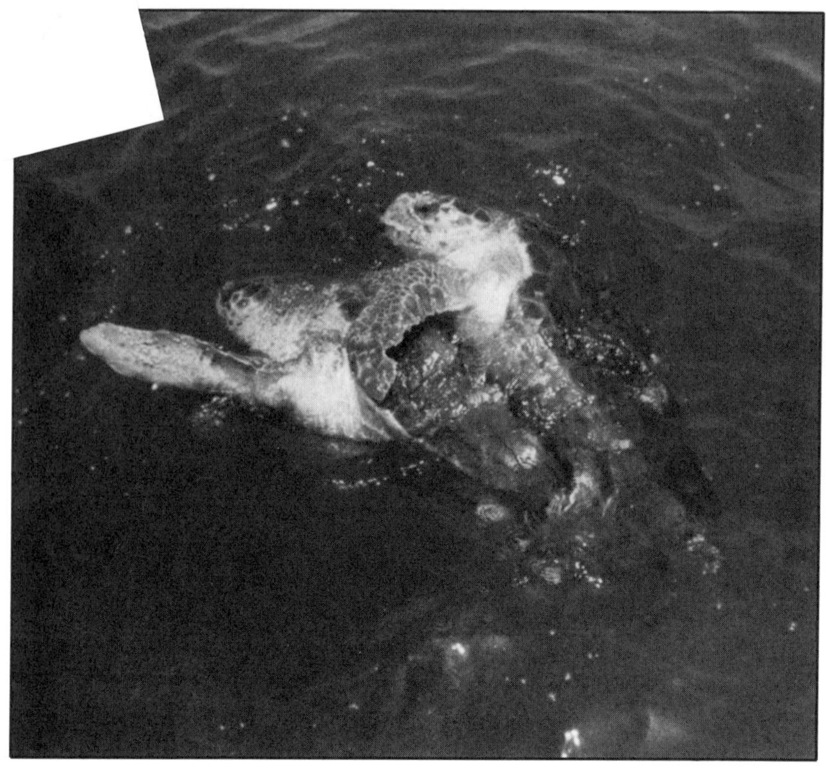

Mating loggerhead sea turtles produce baby turtles that predators like sea birds, raccoons and even snook eat.

Photo by Captain Dale Marler

often more keyed to specific availability of food.

Where live pilchards may work magic on skinny water snook, the fish of deep water may want a lot more. A different presentation, a different bait -- or even, a simple change in how you fish a bait.

But, that's snook fishing. If it were easy nobody would want to do it.

Chapter 8

WINTER FISHING

Some of the best snook fishing of the year occurs during the coldest months. And if you have read this book carefully you know why. One of the keys to catching snook is to find hungry fish in large concentrations.

Snook concentrate to spawn, or if an abundance of food attracts them to an area. But there is nothing that forces snook together as much as weather. Snook can not live in water much below 60 degrees. Hence, they move up into the rivers and creeks during the winter. And, since there are only so many rivers and creeks, cold weather means large concentrations of snook.

There isn't much food for the snook in these backwaters. And that means winter snook are always hungry. Meanwhile, the water in the winter rivers is much dirtier than the crystal seas of the summer grass flats. And there isn't any floating grass in the rivers during the winter.

For all of those reasons cold weather is the absolute best time to catch linesiders on artificial lures and flies. Oh they will eat live shrimp, mullet and other baits. But why waste such an opportunity? Winter snook are suckers for artificials. And catching a fish on a lure or fly may be the most enjoyable method of fishing.

"Weather is everything to fishing," Scott says.

"Weather dictates every thing that snook do. Wind, lack of wind, temperature -- all of those things are much more important to catching snook then the tide, the bait, the phases of the moon or anything else. Weather is everything."

And, during the winter, the weather becomes even more critical to snook. Summer snook are merely reacting to

Small mangrove creeks and the upper reaches of coastal rivers provide havens from the cold for winter snook.

genetic memory patterns when the mercury falls a few degrees. But winter can mean death to snook. Temperature plays a big role in winter fishing.

Sixty degrees is the magic mark for fishing winter snook in the backwaters. When the gulf of Mexico or the Atlantic Ocean approaches that temperature it means that the bays and estuaries where snook live during the temperate months are already far colder, and no place for a snook that wants to see tomorrow.

Deepwater ports and marinas often harbor winter snook, but these areas can also be death traps if a freeze occurs. However, winter snook are thick -- and safe from a freeze -- around any number of power plants where thermal water discharges keep the water warm for the snook despite the weather. But those are not traditional winter fishing grounds for the snook. So the majority of winter snook fishing takes place in the safety of the rivers and creeks.

Sheltered waters don't cool off as much or as fast as open

waters. Meanwhile, the rivers and creeks feature freshwater runoffs that produce heat. And, even though land temperatures are much colder inland than at the coast, springs and rotting vegetation generate heat in the upper reaches of the rivers and creeks.

And that's where winter snook go. Understanding their relationship with warm water is a key to catching them.

Creek mouths, spillways, points of land and sandbars are

This could be an angler's favorite Christmas tree—driftwood adorned with top snook lures. At top left are the Zara Spook, and the lipped diving lure (in this case a Bomber). Below the Bomber on the left is the Rat-L-Trap. A Cotee Jig perches in the middle of the photo with a MirrOlure beneath it. On the right are the fabulous Spinanna and Castana. And on the far right is the old standby—in this case a Bubbas bucktail jig. Lures courtesy of Island Discount Tackle.

all good places to find winter snook for one simple reason. Sure such things wash bait to hungry snook. But runoffs also produce warm water in the creek mouths. Spillways and points provide a collision between water masses. And, when water bodies are forced together friction between water molecules produces heat. Water is also heated when it sits over shallow sandbars and soaks up the winter sun.

The weather may be cold but not the fishing action.

You can also find cold weather snook around downed trees, for rotting vegetation also produces heat, and detritus that produces microscopic food for the small fish and crabs that snook eat during the winter.

In many small creeks and canals linesiders can be found right along the mangroves for many of the same reasons. But, unlike warm weather snook on the flats, winter snook have lots of place to go.

Most rivers and creeks have dozens of rivulets, tiny runoffs that branch off the main tributary. Way up the rivers the influx of freshwater means a change in vegetation that may see marshes of needle or sawgrass. And tidal creeks are usually lined with mangroves, and the little runoffs that are scattered through them.

Such tiny streams mean warm water and food for snook. So, at high tide, they prowl these areas. And that means scattered fish. Snook fishing is much better when the fish are concentrated. And they aren't concentrated during the higher tides.

Consequently, the best time to fish for winter snook is low water. Ironically, spring and summer snook fishing is often better during high tide. But in the winter you want the lowest tide possible.

A new moon, north wind and a cold morning that warms up later on provides the best scenario for winter snooking. North winds make the tide go lower than usual. Cold mornings keep snook from feeding at night. And new moons produce very low tides during the winter. Those things will concentrate hungry snook in the backwaters.

Then all you have to do is fish those points, runoffs, sunken trees, sandbars and spillways to catch snook. Like flats fishing it's important to stay off the areas you want to fish as much as you can. But that can be a problem for fly fishing devotees. It's nice to be 30 or 40 yards off the fish. But few anglers can throw a fly much beyond 100 feet.

Electric trolling motors don't play a large role in most snook fishing scenarios, but they can really help for fly rodding backwater snook. Their chief use here is to hold the boat in a spot without putting down an anchor or banging around a push pole.

Probably the best way to catch a big snook on a fly is to use an electric trolling motor to sneak up on a point. Then you can cast a fly to the other side of the point of land, and the point blocks your presence from the snook.

Large snook are notorious for not taking flies well. But weighted white streamers fished on the offside of river points could set records. Besides the stealth factor, river points often mean that there aren't a lot of obstructions in the water for the snook to tangle a fly line around. The same technique works equally well for bass -- the freshwater equivalent of a snook, and a gamefish you are just as likely to catch during an expedition for linesiders in most snook rivers.

The same scenario can by played out if you are using the lightly weighted balsa plugs. The lipped diving lures such as the Bomber, Rapalas, Rebels, Bang-O-Lures Goldeneyes, and their clones, are outstanding snook lures. But they don't have much casting weight. Light lines can help here, but a paddle or a trolling motor can also help you sneak up on winter snook with a light lure.

There is no better snook bait in the world then a jig. These lead and hair, plastic or feather combinations are responsible for catching more snook than all the live pilchards in the sea.

Jigs can simulate many things. Rapidly retrieving them using the "Florida Whip" makes a good glass minnow imitation. Mean—while, traditional bottom bouncing simulates the crabs, shrimp and sand perch that winter snook eat.

Winter and spring is the only time of year when snook eat blue crabs. They don't eat them out of choice, for snook are not bottom grubbers like redfish. Instead snook eat crabs during the winter because blue crabs also move up river during the cold weather. And that means they are often the only food source in that river. Crabs are also slow moving, easy-to-catch prey. And winter snook must conserve energy by only chasing slow moving food.

On really cold days bouncing a jig in front of a snook's nose is about the only way to get a bite. Trolling with spoons and spoon plugs works the same way, because this also brings a lure just past a snook's nose. But far too many snook are illegally snagged by trollers. So this fishing method borders on the unethical during the winter.

The old silver or red headed Floreo jigs or No-Alibis make outstanding snook lures. The Bubba's Jigs produce terrific white bucktail jigs in the old style. But the plastic tailed jig is

The only drawback to winter snook fishing is the size of the snook. Winter is a good time to catch lots of fish, but most of them will be small like this one. But, even the little ones are fun to catch.

starting to replace bucktail-style lures. Besides white, good colors for jigs include: chartreuse, gold-flake and motor oil. Still white jigs are the standby.

"I think snook can see white farther away than other colors," Moore says.

"Maybe that is one of the reasons ladyfish and pilchards work so well. They both have white sides."

Most of the better plugs also offer white sides. But in the diving plugs Scott favors noisy ones.

"Sometimes the only way to get winter snook to bite is to aggravate them. Snook will kill a ladyfish or needlefish just to kill it. Maybe it is a means of eliminating competition for food, just like African lions will kill hyenas or leopards if they get a chance."

Eliminating a competitor would be even more important to snook during the winter deprivation. Rattling lures are very effective at maddening snook into striking. Perhaps they sound like feeding -- therefore competing -- fish.

Noisy crankbaits like the Rat-L-Trap also allow the angler to cover a lot of water, and using them is a good method for finding winter snook.

Mirrolures also cover the water well. And, while the green and white Mirrolure is a snook killer in the clear waters of spring, the red and white and yellow and red plugs work better in the winter backwaters.

On the warmer days surface lures are good snook getters. And the best lure for aggravating snook that won't bite is the Zara Spook, and its patented "walk the dog" retrieve. Dalton Specials, Devil's Horse lures and the Bagley Jumping Mullet are also good topwater snook baits. Meanwhile, the Boone Spinanna and Castana are terrific snook plugs. They are wonderfully versatile and can be worked as a topwater "walk the dog" type, or as a diving item.

But there is one great trick to catching a winter snook on a surface lure. Since topwater baits tend to aggravate snook the linesider will often attempt to kill this intruder by hitting it with his tail. Most anglers interpret this as a simple missed strike and continue the retrieve. But the snook will turn after it strikes at the lure to see if it has killed the subject of its wrath.

So the retrieve should be stopped after a boil is made on the lure. Just let the plug float there for about 10 seconds then begin barely twitching it. This technique will almost always draw a maddened strike.

The only drawback to winter snooking is the fact that you will catch lots of fish, but most of them will be small and undersized. Its not because there are more small snook in the rivers its just that since all the snook, big and small, are concentrated there, the bigger, more experienced, fish get beaten to the bait a lot. Meanwhile, snook are hermaphroditic and live the first few years of their life as males. Consequently, the smaller males feed much more aggressively than the larger female snook.

You can counter that situation by using large surface lures. The smaller fish will often leave them alone. But they might anger a big snook into biting.

Moving a lot is important for winter fishing. You can sit on snook during the warm months when you are fishing live bait. Eventually they will bite. But lure fishing is different. A snook will seldom eat a lure or fly that you have shown it many times.

If the snook doesn't bite it right away the odds of it biting will go down the more casts you make. A better technique is to move to another area and return later, or change lures.

Snook wallop whitebait with authority. They guzzle grunts with gusto. But there is no finer sight in fishing than watching a big snook explode on a surface lure up the rivers during the winter.

We could talk about lure fishing at any time of the year. But if you really want to catch snook on artificials try the winter. The action will be a lot hotter than the temperature. And you will learn a lot about the snook when you visit the linesider during this phase of his life.

Chapter 9

BRIDGES AND PIERS

Before the first Primadonna, in Scott Moore's teenage years, he began honing his snook fishing talents by fishing from piers and bridges and seawalls. And he perfected those talents long before graduating to his successful guiding career.

In fact, Scott and I both spent most summers of our boyhood fishing off the Rod and Reel Pier on Anna Maria Island, Florida.Later Scott fished for snook at night off the nearby Anna Maria City Pier. And, eventually, Moore would fish from most fishing piers and bridges in the country -- even a couple in the far away regions of Michigan. Scott's wife, Karen, is a native of that state.

Scott Moore is the world's expert on snook for one good reason. Few guides see the snook in as many areas and times of their life cycle as Moore does. There are some very good snook guides who only fish for the linesider during the spring. There are others who only fish for snook in the winter backwaters. And there are those experts who do nothing but chase snook from bridges or piers. But very few snook fishermen have caught fish in all those different ways.

Scott Moore has.

Simple things make for successful fishing off bridges and piers. Little things like the troll-rite bait keeper.

The troll-rite is a yellow jig head designed to be used with live bait -- usually a jumbo shrimp. This device is very effective around piers and bridges because such structures jut out into deep water. And that means lots of current. There-

The troll-rite and live shrimp combination is a deadly bait for snook around bridges and piers.

fore a freelined or weighted bait tends to spin unnaturally in the current. The troll-rite has a slight keel that keeps the bait from turning in the tide.

And Scott thinks the yellow color attracts snook. In Florida shad (menhaden) are a terrific snook bait. However, are hard to catch and difficult to keep alive, so they make a poor bait for most anglers to use. But some bridge fishermen slay snook with shad baits, especially off the Sunshine Skyway Bridge over Tampa Bay. Shad are yellow, and Scott thinks the troll-rite's yellow color may attract snook that are looking for this baitfish.

Some anglers and scientists believe that fish don't see colors. But most anglers don't buy that. And, even if a fish can't tell blue from green, it certainly sees shades and hues. Yellow is one color that stands out for fish, especially in deep or dirty water.

Meanwhile, the jury is still out on whether or not fish can

see colors. Certainly some fish can. Sophisticated research by Dr. Eugenie Clark of the Cape Haze Marine Laboratory (now Mote Marine Lab) during the 1960s proved that lemon sharks could distinguish between colors.

Keep using that yellow troll-rite.

Pier and bridge fishing is often marked by the use of live bait. Artificial lures will catch fish, but most non-boating anglers opt for live bait. And, when you are using live bait from a bridge or pier, presentation is extremely important.

"People sometimes catch snook from piers or bridges just by tossing over a line," Moore says.

"But the better anglers know that these snook are spooky. To catch them you have to get down on all fours and crawl around a pier, looking over the side until you spot some snook. Then you need to drop a bait in the water away from the fish, and gently crawl it up near them. That's the best way to catch pier snook. The same technique works off bridges only you don't have to crawl since you are further away from the fish."

Most snook fishing off bridges and piers is done at night. And that means that shadows can play a key role in properly presenting a bait to a snook.

Most piers have a shadow line that runs parallel to the walkway of the dock. By lying down on the walkway and keeping a bait just on the edge of the shadow line the odds go way up for catching a linesider.

Bridge and pier snook use light in many different ways. One of the oldest tricks for catching fish from a dark structure at night is to lower a lantern from a rope until a brief circle of light falls on the water. The light attracts bait and that entices all manner of gamefish. But the lantern also creates a shadow edge that is more important to the intelligent snook than to other predators.

One summer the Rod and Reel Pier, on Anna Maria Island, was loaded with juvenile scaled sardines. And the tiny bait

High piers and bridges offer good snook fishing for shorebound anglers.

was massed around the dock in dense black schools. Hordes of snook were ganged up at that pier, but they would only sporadically attack the small bait.

That's when some enterprising anglers thought to turn the pier lights out. As soon as everything went dark the snook lit into the small baitfish like rampaging piranhas.

Remember, deep water snook are opportunists. These pier snook knew that the sudden loss of light would leave the bait blind and helpless, and that made for easy pickings. Snook just won't chase bait needlessly. Those snook knew that, sooner or later, the small bait would make a mistake and stray across the shadow line. And, when the lights went out, the snook wasted no time taking advantage of the suddenly blinded bait.

That's why keeping a bait in a shadow line is important to catching pier snook.

Another fact of life for pier snook is their coexistence so close to people who dangle hooks around them, drop weights on them, attempt to illegally spear them and tramp noisily over their heads. Pier snook are much more wary than their counterparts anywhere else.

Consequently, fishing for them late at night when, things are quiet, is often the ticket to catching them.

At other times you must make a dock snook angry in order to get it to bite.

Needlefish are famous baits for pier or bridge snook, not because the snook eats these strange creatures. Instead, needlefish anger gamefish like snook and (barracuda). So these predators tend to attack needlefish and kill them out of spite. A snook will kill a needlefish and just swim around with the spindlebeak in its mouth. Often for hours.

It's clear that they don't eat them. Yet you can make difficult pier snook bite a needlefish. But, since they don't eat

Pier snook can be taken with relatively light tackle. But it takes some skill and a quick hand with a landing net to wrestle a linesider out of the pilings.

them, it's hard to hook a snook using such baits. The angler has to be on the bait and set the hook in such a way as to pull it back into the fish.

Heavy tackle is often necessary for bridge anglers, since catching a snook from a bridge may mean walking the fish the length of the structure until a low spot can be found to land the fish. But most piers are relatively low structures and most dock fishermen use tackle that is far too heavy.

The custom of using heavy cable leaders or 200-pound test monofilament for snook has about stopped. But even a 100-pound mono leader for a pier snook isn't a must. Pier snook can be landed reliably with 25-pound line and 60-pound leaders. And, like snook everywhere, pier snook are getting more and more educated. In clear water spooky pier snook will definitely bite better on lighter line and freelined baits.

Still, it takes a good angler to wrestle a pier snook out of the pilings with light gear.

Pier snook eat many different baits. On the east coast a type of croaker gulfcoasters call a butterfish is one of the hot baits. And silver mullet work on both coasts. Baits for pier snook have to do mostly with the type of forage that is hanging around the pier.

If there are a lot of mullet around then mullet might be the best bait. For if there are no mullet nearby the snook will not be targeting this baitfish, and the appearance of an odd one will seem unnatural to the snook.

That's the reason jumbo shrimp are always good baits around bridges and piers. Shrimp are active in deep water areas at night. And they are attracted to the shadow and light edge that nearly all bridges and piers feature.

The use of deep diving lipped plugs off piers and bridges has picked up in popularity in recent years. And this technique can be quite effective, especially in dirty water. Oddly enough, this is one of the few places for a wire leader in snook fishing. Anglers around the Punta Gorda area catch huge snook around bridges with diving lures and wire leaders. The wire helps keeps the plug down in the current, and the snook has trouble seeing it in the dark anyway.

And live scaled sardines will work around piers and bridges just as they do on the flats. But, since structures often play home to these baitfish most anglers don't use them because they are already thick there. But that's where presentation comes in.

Bait placement is everything when you are fishing off bridges and piers. Not only is it important to keep the bait or lure in front of the snook's nose. But the use of shadow lines and other natural ambush points is also part of presentation.

Boat, seawall or pier, snook fishing changes little from place to place. On the grass flats the edge of a pothole is a natural ambush point for the snook. Meanwhile, a shadow line around a dark pier or bridge can offer the same thing to the linesider.

Understanding the ambush points for the snook can be one of the keys to catching them -- wherever you fish.

Chapter 10

CLIENTS & CATASTROPHES

"It's funny how I first met Scott," longtime client Jay Wiseman says.

"My son and I had gotten into fishing, but we didn't know much about it. So we chartered a south Florida fishing guide during the winter. We caught a few trout, a couple of flounder and managed to luck out (we thought) and catch one snook in the 25-inch class.

"The guide raved about the snook. And since we didn't know any better we were pretty happy too. I was even more impressed when the guide hung the carcass of the snook next to his sign after the fillets were removed. He explained that snook were such rare catches that even what was left of the skin and bones was noteworthy."

But shortly after that Jay Wiseman began to hear rumors of a guide named Scott Moore. They were tales of a fishing guide who caught fish of all kinds in numbers that were unheard of.

But Wiseman was skeptical.

"This was in the 1970s, you see, and that kind of fishing was just not known of then."

But Wiseman booked the new guide anyway. He was told he had a confirmed date to fish.

"No. He was recommended by the right people. No. He didn't need to send a deposit. Just show up at the dock at 7:30."

It seemed like an unorthodox way of doing business. So Jay Wiseman, concerned that he had not heard from this Scott Moore, phoned the fishing guide the night before the trip.

"Yes. He was scheduled. No he did not need to bring bait."

"And that really worried me," Wiseman said.

Many of the south Florida fishing guides he had used insisted that the client buy the bait -- live shrimp, and usually lots of it -- over and above the charter cost.

"Bait will be taken care of," the young fishing guide told Wiseman. "We will catch it in the morning."

Now Jay's fears really began to mount. A guide who doesn't ask for a deposit and doesn't touch bases before a trip. And now one who not only spurns the clients offer to furnish the all important shrimp bait, but wants to catch it as well?

It was a mystery to Jay Wiseman. But it was too late to back out of the charter now. So Jay and his son decided to make the best of what might be a bad decision. At the time he did not know that he was about to be one of the lucky few to get in on Scott Moore's select client list during some of snook fishing's golden years.

All he knew then was that he was going to be fishing with a somewhat untested guide who had unorthodox methods. The morning would not bring much reassurance.

"The first thing Scott began to do was to drive the boat all over the place, then stop and throw out chum for bait. But nothing happened," Wiseman relates.

"We would go here and there and chum and chum, and Scott would suddenly hush us: 'Did you hear a flick there? Did you see a flash?'"

But Wiseman and his son were neophytes to serious fishing. So they had no idea what Scott Moore was talking about. They did not know how to catch live pilchards. They didn't even know what they were. They understood shrimp, perhaps the poorest of baits for snook on the flats.

"So we drove and looked and chummed and listened to ghost flickers and looked for imaginary flashes (or so we thought at the time) until my son started getting nervous. He

Captain Scott Moore nets a nice snook for a client. Netting fish, cleaning them and entertaining the customers are all part of the job of being a professional fishing guide.

kept asking me when we were going to fish. But, by now, I was convinced we were being taken for a ride. And I just wanted to get out of it without a confrontation.

"Finally Scott asked if we had heard a flick."

Of course the Wisemans had not.

"There it is, there's a flash," Scott said, making his cast net to throw. "Now we'll have our bait."

And the Wiseman's began to get very nervous.

"My son said; 'Dad, there's nothing there.'"

By now Wiseman had decided that the strange fishing guide

A happy Scott Moore client shows off a 10-pound snook.

was a madman, and he quietly cautioned his son to humor the fiend.

"The worst of it was the way he would chum for the blasted bait. He couldn't just throw out handfuls. Just little bitty flicks at a time. It just made no sense to anything I knew about fishing."

So the pair decided to favor this lunatic. And when he announced that the unseen bait was ready to net, they privately guffawed.

"Scott threw that net, and we knew his comeuppance was on us. Only lo and behold the castnet was jammed with small silver fishes, flashing and flicking just the way Scott had described them."

"And, now we go fishing," Captain Moore told the Wisemans.

But the day was far from saved.

"After the hours of looking for nonexistent bait we had been ready to write Scott off," Wiseman told me during a drive from Boca Grande to Tampa.

"But we were relaxing a little after he did finally catch some. So we pulled up to a spot and my son and I were eager to get lines in the water. Other guides always fed us that nonsense about how your chances went up the more often you had lines in the water."

But not Scott. Seconds after he had whipped baits around and chummed a few crippled pilchards, Moore told the Wisemans to reel up. They were moving.

"My son started to complain again. And I thought, here we go. But I sat down and just decided to write this experience off and not go with this nut again. That's when Scott did something that really drove us crazy," Wiseman says.

"He took the pushpole and moved the boat, maybe, 10 feet, then put the anchor back down. Well, by now my son and I had both about quit fishing, resigned to this crazy man. But, suddenly, we began to hook a fish on every single cast."

And the Wisemans were treated to a Scott Moore outing. For the rest of the day they caught snook, and trout and redfish on nearly every cast. They finally said "enough" and Moore took them to the dock, weary and happy. And now, decidedly in the Scott Moore camp.

Wiseman's story encapsulates the life of a great fishing guide. The humor, pathos, joy and friendship that a guide develops with his clients takes a certain individual.

There are many great fishermen who don't make particularly good guides. And there are some terrific guides who really don't know much about fishing. Scott is a rare blend of both.

He might not know the taxonomic difference between snook and largemouth bass. But he will tell you what they have in common -- and how to catch either. And he'll do it with good nature and humor. And he does it better than just about anyone else.

But being a fishing guide, even a good one, is not an easy life. You must deal with weather, the occasional problem customers, idiots who follow you around, jet skies, idiots who don't know how to fish and plain old bad luck.

One of the pluses to being a good fishing guide is playing host to famous people. Such assignations are seldom easy for the guide. However, they can up the status of the charterboat person in general. And that can help the guide command greater respect, weed out the lousy customers and command higher fees than the beginners get.

Some of the celebrities that have enjoyed the fishing on the

Scott Moore has entertained many celebrities on board the Primadonna. And while an engine failure doomed a trip with an NFL quarterback Moore did manage to catch Coach Sam Wyche his first snook. Wyche now coaches the Tampa Bay Buccaneers, but he is best known as an offensive genius who created the "no huddle" offense, now used by many pro teams.

Ken Griffith (left) of Houston, Texas had to dodge rain squalls all day. But he and his fishing buddy still boated their limit, under Scott's tutelage.

Primadonna include John Kennedy, Jr., Coach Sam Wyche -- the creator of the National Football League's "no huddle" offense, Florida Governor Bob Martinez and the famous artist Syd Solomon.

It's nice to show a celebrity a great day on the water, after all they might send more business of that kind your way. But Murphy's Law has a habit of dropping in right when a guide has the pump primed with fish and a VIP coming into town.

It happened to Scott Moore in April of 1994. A client called the night before a scheduled trip and asked Moore where they could land a helicopter near Boca Grande. The client had a special guest. His name was Vinny Testaverde, quarterback of the National Football League's Cleveland Browns. Testaverde had started eight seasons for the struggling, yet nearby, Tampa Bay Buccaneers. So this snook fishing trip was something of a homecoming for him.

And Scott was on lots of hungry snook. A client had caught one the day before that had measured 40 inches in length -- an April fish that weighed close to 30-pounds.

So they found a place to land the helicopter. And with a multi-million-dollar-a-year quarterback in tow Scott set out to show Vinny Testaverde what real sport was all about.

Only it never happened.

Two hundred yards from the dock the motor broke down. And that was the end of the trip with a quarterback many believe will play in the Super Bowl one day.

Boat breakdowns can kill you but weather can sometimes work to the advantage of a guide like Scott Moore. In April of 1992 a terrible rainstorm struck the west coast of Florida dumping as much as 16-inches of precipitation on the coast in ten hours.

The result was heavy flooding, messy roads, downed power lines, and filthy dirty water that should have precluded all snook fishing for more than a week.

Unfortunately, Scott had a client in town from Houston Texas. His name is Ken Griffith. But he's more than just a client. He's a longtime friend of both authors of this book. And he had brought his boss along to show off the Scott Moore magic.

Coming from Houston the pair had no idea the kind of weather visited on the Florida snook grounds. And I cautioned them to forget that morning's trip. Over a long breakfast Scott told them that they would have to see what the weather did, and even if it allowed them to get out, they probably would not be able to catch bait.

But these guys had just roared in from Houston. And they were itching to get on the water. I didn't envy Scott taking an old high school pal and his boss on a snook fishing trip under those conditions.

No point in trying to catch whitebait in that syrupy coffee.

Instead Moore bought live shrimp, found a pocket of cleaner water, took advantage of the fact that no one else was bothering the snook. And I think they caught 40.

It isn't the catches of 100 snook per trip when all is right and you might expect such a thing that has elevated Scott Moore to legendary status as a guide. Rather it's catching 40 -- or four -- when no one else would even attempt to fish that turns that trick.

But being a fishing guide isn't all fishing. Some of it has to do with being an engaging person. In the outdoor writing business I see lots of different guides and talk to lots of clients about fishing guides. The two things I hear most in praise of a guide are: A. He works hard: and: B. He has a good personality.

I'd tell you about Scott Moore's third grade class at Jessie P. Miller School if that would explain his personality. But there are parents and teachers still alive who might develop health problems if we went into those details.

Suffice it to say that Scott, in fact most great guides, still have a bit of the boy in them. It's one of the things that makes them engaging fellows to spend a day in a boat with. And it's one of the things that keeps them focused; able to adapt quickly to the everchanging world that is the marine environment.

I also think that boy-like quality in good guides is something that is appealing more and more to women anglers. In the past fishing guides were serious, gruff and committed men. And their clients were too. But there is room for the serious pursuit of angling along with the lighter side.

A classic case involved a trip I had with Scott along with a lady friend named Cindy Maggio. Cindy hadn't fished much. Yet Scott had found a bunch of king mackerel, bonito (little tuna) and big Spanish mackerel. Meanwhile, the women's line class records in the lighter categories was wide open on those fish. So we thought we'd get Cindy a record.

Jane Sammons of Huntsville, Alabama, shows off her woman's world record snook in the eight-pound line class. It's one of two snook records that have been set on the Primadonna. Scott Moore set the two-pound record himself with a snook that was later released alive.

Only trouble was, Cindy did not take kindly to my more serious coaching. She was an inexperienced angler, but -- like a lot of women -- she still did not want to be told what to do. So Scott left her alone. And, after a few fearful glares, I did too.

Well Cindy hooked a potential world record bonito on about four pound test line. And after cautions to hold the rod up, etc. were met with baleful glances, we left her to her own devices.

We were, after all, engaged in catching these offshore heavyweights on fly rods until we heard Cindy squeak.

"What'll I do?" she asked. "I don't have any string left."

The bonito had stripped the reel of line. But there was so much slack that the belly in the line acted as drag and had worn the fish out. That's when the instructions on pumping and reeling and keeping the rod up began to make sense.

I might have gotten in a fight with her over the thing. But Scott didn't. That's one reason he's the fishing guide and I'm the guy who writes about fishing guides.

For Scott Moore, fishing is fishing. It's the same thing to Scott to catch a six-year-old kid his first snook as it is to set an International Gamefish Association World Record (he has set two such records with snook). It's the same thing to Scott to watch an inexperienced woman angler feel her way to master status, as to guide a veteran to a trophy mount.

Fishing is fishing to this guide. It's what makes him in demand and I think it's what makes him good.

A guide who only chases trophy tarpon, or permit on fly, or a guide who looks merely for line class world records doesn't see the entire spectrum of the marine environment. Being a great guide means being on the water as much as you can be in as many different situations as possible.

The clients come and the catastrophes go. But guides like Scott live on the water regardless of either.

And they build on each other. One of the things that has

made Scott Moore a great fishing guide is his clients. It's anglers like Bob Sammons and Phil Alessi and Andy Massaro, Mac Greco and Stanley Glen -- and so many others -- that have enabled Scott to experiment. The guide had to be good in the first place, but having good people to fish with helps as well.

Without clients like that a guide is just another fisherman.

Chapter 11

TRANSITION FISHING

Anybody who has read this book up to now can catch snook that are locked into a pothole on a grass flat in May. That same everyday Joe can read the chapter on winter fishing and fill his limit in the backwaters when the cold winds blow.

But, now we come to the chapter that separates the men from the boys. For catching snook that are in transition may be the most difficult of FISHING arts to perform.

Snook are in transition for many reasons at many times of the year. Transition snook are moving fish. They may be in transition because of a tide change that has them moving from one water depth to another. But snook do that every day during the spring and summer. So transition on a flat more aptly applies to an extreme condition that may move them unnaturally onto or off of a flat.

North winds and big moons can make for transitional situations in flats fishing. But transition fishing more properly refers to fish that are on the move due to environmental conditions. Snook are in transition as they make their way from the cold weather refuges to their summer haunts. Transition also happens during the fall as they return to their winter homes. But transition can also occur as fish move from one area to another.

And calamities can cause transitional situations. In recent years both sudden red tides and early cold snaps have produced transitional situations that have produced unusual, and sometimes outstanding fishing.

Scott had such a situation occur in Boca Grande in November of 1993. Several early cold fronts had developed into unseasonably cold temperatures, and most of the snook had scurried off the flats and into canals and other backwaters for warmth. Then the cold fronts stopped and the temperature climbed back up, and the snook began poking their noses back out onto the flats.

But another severe cold front came swooping down and caught the snook out on the flats. And that meant they had to move and move fast. It was a classic case of transition.

"I was running along in a place where I had never seen a snook before," Scott says.

"The main reason I have a tuna tower on my boat is for tarpon fishing. Towers are not necessary for snook fishing. Still I tend to run the boat from the tower even if I am on a flat. So I just happened to see hundreds of snook in this place where they had never been before."

So Moore turned around and started fishing. For a half an hour his clients caught a snook on every cast. Then it was over. Nothing. Scott climbed into the tower again and circled around looking for the snook. But they were all gone. A couple of hours later the temperature began to drop rapidly -- just as those snook knew it would.

By accident Scott had caught those fish in the peak of transition. But you can find them in this kind of flux deliberately. And the thing about transitional snook is that they will often bite much better than other fish. For transitional snook have certain demands that other fish don't have.

Transition fish are moving, and with serious purpose. They may be fleeing cold weather, or moving towards the estuary in order to find food after the winter deprivation. Those scenarios are typical for spring and fall fishing.

But transition can occur for other reasons. Often a flat that had few snook on it will suddenly be full of linesiders that were not there before. And they are usually hungry. Not all the snook leave the backwaters at the same time. Some fish will stay up in the rivers and creeks till the last minute before

Red tides and sudden freezes can kill snook and other fish, but they can also cause transitional fishing situations that can produce terrific action, often for big snook.

moving out to the flats. Meanwhile, snook may stay in an area until they eat all the food that is there. Then they must go somewhere else and that accounts for suddenly finding warm weather snook where none were before. It's because they just arrived.

If you can find snook like these it can mean a really hot bite. Fish in transition have more energy demands on them than homesteaders. They will have just made a long journey, and that requires energy. And that creates a demand to feed quickly.

Meanwhile, snook that are in transition often behave strangely.

"I was fishing with Mark Harrison and my son Justin a couple of years ago when we were able to really experience snook in transition," Scott says.

"We were fishing a channel that leads into a trailer park. And the channel had recently been blasted out to widen it, and that had exposed some jagged edges of limestone. So

Transitional snook are on the move, either because of a calamity, shortage of food or a simple change in the seasons that sends them from their winter to summer homes.

they had sunken a bunch of extra pilings in the channel to ward boats away from the rocks. It was loaded with snook, but landing one with all those pilings around would be another story."

But the trio hooked and caught 14 snook in about 40 minutes and never lost a single linesider to a piling.

"The next day we went back and hooked three straight snook. And each one wrapped around a piling and broke off. Those were traveling snook. When we found them they had just gotten there. They did not know their surroundings yet, and they did not know the pilings were there. But they learned."

Red tides occur regularly along the Florida gulfcoast, occasionally off the east coast and, sometimes, in Texas. A red tide is caused when microscopic organisms called dinoflagellates experience a sudden, intense population explosion. During red tides the dinoflagellate count soars from the normal of a few hundred per liter of water to over a million organisms per liter.

The organisms give off powerful poisons when they die. And when millions die at a time the level of poison is so great that fish and other marine animals are killed en masse.

Red tides kill tons of mullet, redfish, black drum, grunts, catfish and other slow moving bottom feeders. It would kill snook too. But snook are perhaps the most intelligent of all gamefish. They have an uncanny knack of escaping most red tides. And the fast break from the beaches -- where the poison hits the hardest -- to the safety of the backwaters means some serious transitional fishing for snook anglers.

In 1993 a red tide outbreak off Sarasota saw all manner of gamefish swarm into Tampa Bay. The bay was especially

One of the best spots in the world to find snook in transition is the old railroad trestle over the Myakka River at El Jobean. The trestle marks the halfway point for linesiders that are moving from their summer homes on the beaches to their wintering grounds up the rivers. The trestle also features good structure and monster snook.

loaded with big sharks. These animals also are intelligent enough to avoid red tides. But they usually go offshore. The 1993 bloom apparently caught a bunch of sharks near shore and they decided to go into the bay instead of running offshore.

The snook did the same thing. And, suddenly, places that had been empty of snook for weeks were chock full of them.

But those are extreme cases of finding snook in transition. Usually you find those fish by luck, though keeping a sharp lookout for such things can really pay off.

In most cases of transition fishing things are much more predictable. Snook can be found in the same areas between February and May that they can be found between September and December. In the spring they are moving out of the backwaters and heading towards the coast. In the fall the opposite occurs.

The three-month periods of transition each fall and spring reflect the fact that the linesiders don't all make the move at the same time. And some snook move slower than others.

Snook are like wild ducks when they move. Ducks move south each winter to avoid the deprivation of winter. But if those ducks find a nice cornfield or flooded cropland they may tarry late into winter. Some of them just give up the idea of migrating whatsoever if the food is there and the winter isn't too harsh. So it is with snook as well.

If moving snook happen upon an area with a lot of bait (like glass minnows) they may hole up and delay the trip up or down river. And, if some serious cold fronts aren't forthcoming right away, those snook may just skip the trip up river, particularly if there is a deep water marina or a canal nearby to hide in when a big cold front comes along.

Snook that overwinter in creeks, canals and marinas are not nearly as cooperative as those whose destination is the far reaches up the rivers. The snook that overwinter near the coast don't have to travel nearly as far as river snook. So the

Bruce Manson strains to hold onto this large snook. The big linesider was a fish in transition making its way from the winter backwaters to its summer home. Such snook are often big, and hungry.

energy demand on them is much less.

To succeed on transitional snook you want to target the snook that are heading up into the backwaters, and that means moving in that direction yourself.

Good places to find hungry, traveling snook are creek and bayou mouths, docks, old pilings and submerged pipes, sandbars, sea walls and the mouths of major rivers and bays. If you can find a subdivision with canals in it they make for great snook fishing if they are on the way up the rivers.

The canals of Anna Maria Island, Saint Petersburg Beach and other barrier islands have plenty of snook in them. But they don't bite well because they are near food sources and they haven't had to travel far.

But the canals around Punta Gorda and North Port are outstanding snook waters. They ought to be, they mark the halfway point for snook that intend to overwinter in the upper reaches of the Peace River. And those fish have already made quite a journey.

Transitional snook probably make the best targets for artificial lures. You can often find them in deep, open waters free of the floating grass that makes lure fishing difficult on grass flats. Yet, unlike winter fishing, catching snook in transition gives you a better shot at catching a large fish on a lure.

As we mentioned in the chapter on winter fishing lots of small snook are caught in the winter due to the fact that all the snook are concentrated together. But snook that are on the move often means schools of nothing but large fish. So fishing transitional snook is often the best chance to catch a big one on a lure or fly.

And the transition fish hasn't forgotten his intricate relationship with the scaled sardine. So pilchard imitations like the blue and silver Rat-L-Trap or the green and white Mirrolure often work magic on these fish. Spoons are also effective on moving snook.

Transition fishing in the spring means fishing the same areas as the fall, but in reverse as the fish move towards the coast. But, in the spring, it isn't so important to find snook that are going on a long journey. All snook in the U.S. face starvation during the winter. So spring fish are *all* hungry.

And that means the canal mouths on barrier islands and the shorelines adjacent to marinas and other deepwater basins are good places to find snook that are in transition during the spring. And that's another good place to use artificial lures.

Most anglers start fishing for mackerel when the snook start to move up river. But a snook guide has to fish for them wherever they go, before they go, while they move, and, after they get there.

Transition fishing may be the toughest way to catch snook. But it is often a key to finding big, hungry fish. The big trick is finding them.

Transition snook are not found over clear, shallow, water. So you can not see the fish; you can't look for them with your eyes. You have to look for signs that they are there. The presence of glass minnows is one such sign. But finding transition snook is mostly a matter of fishing for them.

Chapter 12

LIGHT TACKLE TACTICS FOR BIG FISH

At the heart of modern snook fishing is the use of light tackle. But it wasn't always that way. During the 1950's, 60's and 70's most snook anglers used heavy tackle.

The law that made snook a protected gamefish and stopped legal commercial exploitation of this animal did several things. First, that late 50's ordinance changed the way all of Florida's gamefish were looked at. It set the pattern for protection for many sportfish and led to the snook symposiums, and -- finally -- moves to tightly control harvest of marine gamefish in Texas, Florida and most coastal states. But gamefish status for snook also helped create the mythos surrounding the linesider.

When snook became illegal to buy and sell they achieved legendary status with gourmets. Since you could not go to the store and buy snook fillets the only way you could eat them was to catch them yourself or know somebody who did. Or, buy them on the black market.

In the 60's and 70's a huge black market for snook existed. Rogue commercial fishermen routinely netted snook and sold them as scamp grouper. For both the snook and the scamp have black veins running through the flesh. The veins of most grouper species are red.

What the netters did not get was left up to the handful of anglers who knew how to catch snook. And many of them were no better than the illegal netters.

In the 60's and 70's snook were big dollar gourmet items. Everybody who was anybody wanted to serve snook at their parties. After all, since you could not buy snook at the store, it had a limitless value. And serving snook became a status symbol for the smart set in the southeast.

And that scenario led to the use of heavy tackle by most snook anglers.

Snook are often found adjacent to mangroves or other structure and the first thing they do when hooked is to race for that cover in order to cut the line on barnacle encrusted roots. So if you wanted to keep snook -- and in those days everybody did -- it made sense to use lines as heavy as 40-pound test, stout rods and heavy duty bait casting reels.

This was the heyday of the "fish hog" and he measured his success, not by an enjoyable day on the water, but by how many snook bodies he could stack up and hide from the

Doubleheaders with light tackle require oustanding angler efforts, and coordination with the captain. Scott Moore pioneered such light tackle tactics with snook in the 1960s.

Most anglers realize that spotted sea trout like this one have soft mouths and must be handled delicately or the hook will tear free. But snook are often lost to pulled hooks also.

Marine Patrol.

And that's the way it was in the 70's. Snook weren't gamefish. They were meat. And the poachers, that masquer-aded as snook anglers, then, used heavy tackle to load up with as many of them as they could.

Scott Moore changed all that with his light tackle revolution. But he could not have done it without experimenting with the light gear and devising ways to catch big snook on light line.

Today everybody uses light tackle for snook. Yet there are still many misconceptions about snook gear.

The most important piece of equipment for catching big snook on light tackle is the rod. Scott uses long stiff rods for several reasons.

First of all the whitebait that is so important to a successful snook trip between March and October can be easily thrown off when casting. Also catching snook over the clear shallow grass flats means keeping the boat as far from the fish as possible. Tuna towers spook flats snook. Boat hulls spook flats snook. Anglers wearing the wrong color of shirt or hat really spook snook.

Yet if you fish a tower boat, or have customers who show up at the dock wearing a pink shirt, there aren't a lot of things you can do about those problems, except stay as far from the fish as possible.

This closeup shows the delicate cartilage of a snook's mouth. Hooks can tear easily if they wedge into the soft sides of the jaw. And a lot of snook are lost to pulled hooks when this membrane tears. So it's important to fight a snook carefully.

That's where the long, stiff rods come in handy. Such poles will cast a bait or lure a country mile with little effort. And that means throwing off fewer baits. Scott has experimented with several rods, and many will work. But his personal favorites are made by Daiwa, Penn and G. Loomis.

The long stiff rod is also a valuable tool when fighting the fish. Snook are famous for their fighting abilities. Hooked snook make strong runs. Their aerial displays would embarrass a sailfish. They use every part of their marine home to help dislodge a hook. And they usually succeed.

Snook have tough mouths compared with a trout, flounder or members of the mackerel family. Yet a snook's mouth isn't anywhere near as tough as the mouth of a permit, redfish or tarpon. The cartilage in a snook's mouth tears easily. Snook are lost to pulled hooks more than just about any other fish.

Consequently, Scott likes his anglers to take it easy on hooked snook and wear them out away from the boat. If you bring a green snook close to the boat the sudden burst of power that it puts on when it spots the vessel will often result in the hook pulling free.

The long rod also helps in fighting the snook gently. By keeping the rod between the ten and two o clock positions the angler can put steady, easy pressure on the fish without a lot of effort. Shorter rods mean more work for the angler and, therefore, the greater chance for a mistake.

The long rod also helps when the fish jump. Due to the ease that a snook's mouth tears Scott has developed a system for fighting these gamefish that parts company with techniques used for fighting most fish.

Tarpon, marlin and other aerial speedster present specific problems for the angler. When these gamefish jump their speed doubles as they soar out of water. Without the burden of water friction to slow it down a leaping tarpon's speed dramatically increases. And that can result in the line breaking, the hook being thrown, or the fish landing on a tight line -- which also results in a lost fish.

To combat this problem veteran tarpon anglers bow and point the rod straight at the jumping silver king. But Scott says that's the wrong thing to do with snook.

"First of all, a lot of snook are hooked in very shallow water on light line. And that means you often can not tell the fish is going to jump until it's too late," Moore explains.

"But, even if you know he's going to jump, pointing the rod at the fish creates slack line. And if the fish is hooked in certain parts of the mouth the hook will most likely have begun to tear in the softer cartilage. If you give him slack line he will easily throw the hook."

Instead Moore insists that the proper way to address jumping linesiders is to pull back gently on the rod when the fish takes to the air. This technique helps keep slack out the line and frustrates the snook's efforts to throw the hook. It's a very good technique for fly fishermen to master because the belly in the fly line also helps take up slack as the rod is pulled back.

But pulled hooks are often the least of a snook angler's concerns. There is no gamefish on Earth more famous for using its environment in the battle with an angler.

The biggest snook I have ever hooked was at the mouth of the Manatee River with Scott Moore and Bob Sammons of Huntsville, Alabama. I hooked it on a big shrimp when these river fish were spurning whitebait, and it ran straight out into the river.

We all believe it was over 40-pounds. And Moore and Sammons have put snook in the boat that big. This one was a monster and while it wallowed out in the channel I waded after it with visions of line test world records dancing in my head.

Way out there, in chest deep water, someone had dumped a bunch of concrete cinder blocks a long time ago, and I stumbled on one while I was fighting the snook.

After the initial run that big snook came barreling straight towards me, seeking out those cinder blocks. I kept her out of the concrete three times. But the snook finally won the game and cut me off on the sharp edges of the cement.

How that snook knew, and remembered, that those cinder blocks were there is a mystery to me. But stories like that are just one of the examples of the terrific intelligence of this gamefish.

Count on a hooked snook to know where every piling, mangrove root or oyster rock can be found. And count on them to go there after the hookup occurs.

For this reason battling a snook presents a lot of problems for the angler. Again, the long rod helps put pressure on a snook that is racing to the bushes. But technique can also keep a fish out of the mangroves as well.

Scott uses a lot of fighting tactics that were developed by anglers in the Florida Keys for fighting big tarpon with a fly rod. These tactics were developed by fly fishermen, like Billy Pate, in order to whip tarpon quickly on light tackle, before the silver king can catch its second wind. But Scott has adapted these techniques to stop snook from getting to the bushes.

If a snook heads for the mangroves the obvious thing to do is to apply pressure to stop him. But if you put on too much pressure the light line will break. Not enough, and the snook makes it to the bushes, with the same result. It's a tricky game.

But by using the "down and dirty" fighting method developed by Pate the angler can sometimes roll the snook over or turn him long enough to wear him down and dissuade the fish from the mad dash to the mangroves.

The "down and dirty" is accomplished by sticking the rod down into the water alongside the boat and pulling on the snook from the side. Pulling to the side is very important for stopping the mangrove express. The rod should never be held up. You can't turn a snook over on his back, but you can, sometimes, pull him to the right or left.

"And you don't ever, ever want to get straight with the fish. If you do that, it's over." Moore says.

Even a little lady like Dottie Gray can master giant snook on light tackle if the proper technique is used.

Getting straight with a snook that is going to the mangroves means allowing the fish to get an angle on the angler. To keep snook away from cover there should be an arrow straight line between the fish and angler. If the snook starts to angle away the angler needs to move in order to stay on line with the fish.

If a snook destined for the bushes gets an angle on the rod wielder it means maximum pressure can not be applied to the fish. And that usually means another ball of fishing line added to the mangrove decor.

Scott Moore uses Daiwa and Penn spinning reels. And he likes lines testing between four and 10-pound test. Anything heavier negates the long casts that are important to successful snook fishing on the flats.

Fly and baitcasting gear is best left up to the individual angler. But Scott uses a Sage fly rod and Valentine reel. Scientific Anglers also makes terrific and inexpensive fly fishing gear. And there are all kinds of top dollar fly equipment. Probably the most well known is the Billy Pate Special -- an outstanding fly reel, but one that's a bit pricey for many.

And Moore likes to load his reels with fairly limp monofilament like Berkley's Trilene Solar and XT. Triple Fish Camo is also a good line for snook. Fishing the flats is tough on fishing lines and hardy lines like Ande stand up well. But limp lines allow much longer casts.

Whatever line, reel, or rod that you use, and whether you pitch flies or whitebait to snook, one thing is clear. Snook and light tackle belong together. And it doesn't look like the meat fishing of the bad old days will ever intrude upon the linesider again.

Chapter 13

TEN FISHING SECRETS

Besides the scaled sardine there is one other type of migratory baitfish that the snook enjoys a unique relationship with. This food source is one of several species of baitfish that goes by the common name of glass minnow.

Schools of tiny anchovies, silver sides and juvenile scaled sardines make up dense rafts of tiny transparent fishes that provide terrific forage for the snook. But, unlike adult pilchards, the inch-long glass minnows are far too small to have any value as a bait for snook. They are so little that even catching them in a bait net would be quite a feat. And, even if they did achieve enough size to use as a bait, glass minnows are very delicate creatures that die easily.

But snook love them. And understanding the relationship between the snook and the glass minnow is a key to catching snook, particularly those in transition.

Early spring and fall snook often rely heavily on glass minnow forage. If snook have plenty of glass minnows to eat, then the demand to seek out the schools of scaled sardines is not so great. And, unlike whitebait, glass minnows can tolerate brackish waters. Hence, glass minnows can sometimes be found in the rivers and bays. The appearance of glass minnows far up into the estuary probably accounts for the ability of some small snook to remain in the river systems year round.

If snook are actively feeding on glass minnows they will sometimes refuse a live scaled sardine. But, when snook target these small baits it makes them suckers for small jigs and flies. Scott once found a school of snook free jumping in glass minnows off Little Gasparilla Island, and his client caught

Even big snook love tiny glass minnows. And watching out for this small baitfish is a big secret to catching more snook.

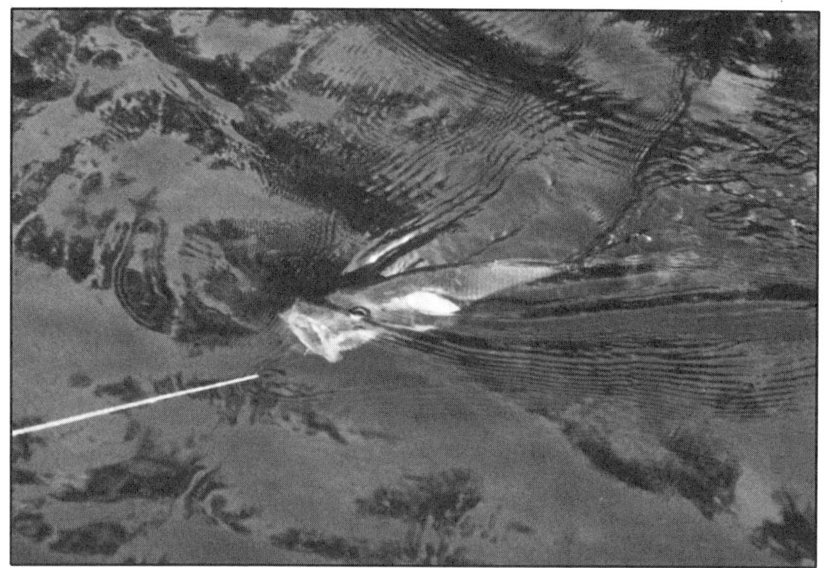

Snook may sleep, but when you wake them up and get them in a biting mood they are all fight. The linesider doesn't know grogginess once he feels the bite of the hook.

more than 20 fish in the 10-pound class on flies. Snook that size are notoriously hard to catch on the long wand. But lunker snook that are savaging glass minnows eat flies with gusto.

Glass minnows can also help you find snook if you can't see them. If the water is dirty or the snook are in deep water the presence of these small baitfish usually means snook are around. And glass minnows will also hold snook in an area.

Ware's Creek is a tributary off the Manatee River that bisects downtown Bradenton, Florida. Yet this cosmopolitan water body has been a snook mecca for 50 years. The reason is glass minnows.

The minnows swim up into Ware's Creek because the abundant nutrient outflow from sewage systems and suburban fertilizer runoff stimulates phytoplankton blooms that the glass minnows feed upon. Often the minnows will swarm into the shallower portions of the creek where snook are loathe to go.

Perhaps the biggest snook secret of all is to learn how to use the Solunar Tables to utilize key feeding periods. With snook there are many different ways to use feeding periods to the angler's advantage.

But that doesn't deter the linesiders. They wait in the mouth of the creek until a big rain or an extra low tide forces the glass minnows out of the creek. Then the feeding begins. Because of the glass minnows, this urban stream still produces some of the finest bank fishing for big snook in the nation.

An easy way to fish it is to cruise along in a car and look for the tell-tale flicker of glass minnows on the surface of the water. If the minnows are there the snook won't be far behind.

So the NUMBER ONE FISHING SECRET is to look for glass minnows. Even if you are going to use shiners for bait (unfortunately glass minnows won't fit on a hook) the presence of large schools of glass minnows in a bay will also mean snook in that area as well.

SECRET NUMBER TWO is that fish sleep. Nobody ever mentions it, but a snook, or any other sedentary fish has to rest. And that explains a lot about fish that won't bite.

"I can't tell you how many times I've poled up on snook that were lying on the bottom and not moving," Scott says.

"Many times you will actually have to poke them with the push pole to get them to move, and then, they just sort of move to the side and settle back down. Those fish are sleeping."

Sleeping fish are not suspended in the water column halfway from the top to the bottom. Suspended fish are usually hungry. But sleeping snook are often found tight on the bottom. And will usually refuse a bait.

Because the snook of spring and summer must meet the ancient needs and gorge on the migratory baitfish, they feed around the clock. If it is a full moon or a school of pilchards or glass minnows happens to blunder into a snook lair at night, then linesiders become great night time feeders. If that's the case the snook will need to rest the next day. It may not be sleep as we humans know it, but fish definitely rest.

A good tactic for sleeping fish is to abandon them to their slumber and pursue more active snook. Yet those snoozing fish will be bunched up. And, when they do wake up they are usually hungry. So leaving sleeping fish also means returning later and trying them again.

But you can also wake sleeping snook up. By poking them with a pushpole or banging on the boat or revving the engine you can force the fish out of their lethargy. Then heavy chumming with whitebait will often create a feeding frenzy.

Unfortunately, the same tactics might also send those rudely awakened linesiders scurrying from the area. So you have to know when to try waking them. Scott lets them sleep unless there are a lot of them, or a feeding period is coming up.

The NUMBER THREE FISHING SECRET may be the biggest one of them all. To catch snook consistently you must under-

Learning how the wind affects the tides in the mangrove/grass flat country and what wind does to fishing is another key to succcessful fishing. Guess the wind and tide wrong and you might be spending the night in the mangroves with the mosquitoes.

Photograph of mangrove backcountry by Jack Elka.

stand how to use the Solunar Tables. These charts of fish and game feeding periods, created by John Alden Knight more than half a century ago, have many uses. Today there are many Solunar Table clones around. But Knight was the originator of this system more than 50 years ago.

To a deer hunter the major feeding periods mean religiously hunting during those times. But to the snook angler they have different applications.

These tables of feeding periods use the position of the moon and the sun to indicate when wildlife will be most active and likely to feed. Major and minor feeding periods work like clockwork on some fish, notably tarpon and largemouth bass. But the snook is so dependent on environmental factors that you have to know how to apply the feeding periods to this fish.

One of the ways to use these tables is with sleeping fish. If you are coming up on a major feeding period that might be the time to wake the fish up. But, if you are two hours away from such a feeding frenzy it might be better to let them sleep.

The feeding period can also save a snook fishing trip when bad weather has the snook off their feed. And, using the major feeding periods can be a guide to knowing when to chum for snook. Over chumming can ruin snook fishing. But if you chum during a feeding period, you will be liable to get a response.

The NUMBER FOUR FISHING SECRET is to use crippled pilchards for chum in order to track fish. By chumming and watching for the telltale "pop" a snook makes when it eats this bait you can find out where the fish are and which way they are going. This allows you to follow them as they move. And it means less use of the motor to find them.

FISHING SECRET NUMBER FIVE also involves the use of the Solunar Tables. Catching bait, in the form of live scaled sardines, is often the hardest part of serious snook fishing. Early in the morning cooler water temperatures often means whitebait will not chum well. And that can make for a tough morning of fishing.

Meanwhile, a snook angler may have to catch bait several times during the day. Yet it is important that the bait be netted quickly, or the angler may be missing the best part of the tide for catching snook.

Scott suggests the angler stop what he is doing if a feeding period is coming up. If there is bait close by, and the angler needs it, then the feeding period may be the best time to catch all the bait that will be needed quickly. If you can leave the snook and catch the bait in 10 minutes, you will be back in time to take advantage of the feeding period with the linesiders as well. But you have to have bait, if you want to catch lots of snook.

Using the feeding period to catch bait quickly means taking a chance. But such chances are the things that make great fishing guides.

Understanding the effect of the wind is the NUMBER SIX FISHING SECRET. Wind direction probably affects snook more than any other fish. Wind affects all fish on a flat because of how it changes a tidal movement. South and west winds tend to push the tide up, hold it there longer, and make for a much longer high tide.

This scenario can work several ways. It can mean great fishing, especially if it occurs during a major Solunar Period, because it keeps the fish on the flat longer. And since they go there to feed anyway, this may mean longer exposure to hungry snook.

On the other hand, south and west winds can force the tide so high that it can spread the fish out on a flat, sending many of them far up under the mangroves, and away from your baits. South and west winds work best on slower tides. If they occur during the big tides of the full and new moons, they can spread snook out on a flat.

Meanwhile, north winds make the tides go lower than normal. And this phenomena can send snook scurrying from the flats sooner than usual. Those are the times when anglers accidentally run over snook that were far from where they should have been. Yet, such a scenario can also work to your advantage.

Scott and I fished together one day under just such conditions. A big tide and south wind had the snook scattered all up under the mangroves and we could not buy a bite. Then the wind turned to the north and the tide started out. Still no snook anywhere.

We finally decided to look for them on the outer bar, a quarter mile from the mangroves, despite the fact that the tide was still outrageously high. We found them and caught them by the score for about twenty minutes before they dropped all the way out. But they had left that flat the moment the wind and the tide turned together. For snook, like most gamefish, are quite paranoid about getting stuck on a shallow flat when a big tide starts roaring out.

Northeast winds are poor breezes for fishing. Such winds often tend to make the gamefish tentative about biting. They will nip at baits at such times rather than busting them with authority. But there is one wind scenario that is especially deadly to snook fishing.

"The worst possible weather condition for snook is constant wind," Scott says.

"There is nothing worse than having two or three or more days of wind that always blows from the same direction, say all south, or all east. That will kill snook fishing."

Rather the best fishing occurs during normal wind patterns. In most coastal areas around the world that means an offshore wind during the morning with an afternoon seabreeze that dies at night. Weather systems moving through will change that scenario. Yet, even in the depth of winter, the wind patterns (between cold fronts) resemble those of summer.

Avoiding constant winds will mean better days for snook anglers.

SECRET NUMBER SEVEN involves the use of artificial lures. Changing the hooks on lures like the Rebel, Bagleys' Jumping Mullet, Rapala and Goldeneye can really up the odds on catching linesiders with these phonies.

These lures are designed for largemouth bass. And snook are simply much tougher on small hooks then bass are. Not only will a snook straighten factory hooks, but larger hooks also make the lures work better for snook.

Meanwhile, avoid showing any lure or fly to a snook more than once or twice. Don't cast to the same place more than two times. And, if you have covered the water and not drawn a strike, then either move or change lures. Snook are one of the most intelligent of fish. We can think of no other gamefish that knows where the mangroves are and how to get to them even if he is hooked far out of sight of them. If you show them the lure too much, they will figure it out.

The NUMBER EIGHT FISHING SECRET involves winter fishing. In chapter nine we went into detail about where to find winter snook. But there is one trick for finding winter snook that will pay for years. Yet it can only be accomplished about once every five years.

During the rare freezes that kill and cripple snook take advantage of the early morning ice to visit the spots where snook spend the winter. These include deepwater ports, marinas, canals, creeks and up the rivers themselves. Then look for floating, cold-stunned snook. The vast majority of these snook will be revived later in the day when the sun comes out.

And most of them will survive. But by seeing where the floaters are you will know where to find winter snook for years to come. Just go to the spot where the fish floated during the freeze and there will be hungry snook there when the weather moderates.

FISHING SECRET NUMBER NINE involves knowing when to fish. The four-tide days of the stronger moons are by far the best times to fish for any kind of gamester. Four-tide days are better because they give the angler more opportunities to get in on "the bite."

If the bite occurred on the flat during a quarter moon tide, then you only get one shot at it during a two-tide day. But four-tide days mean more tide changes. And since snook feed during current exchanges, more tide changes mean more chances for hungry snook.

"Also try to fish the new moon," Scott says.

"Snook will take advantage of the full moon to feed at night. So the new moon often means better fishing, especially in the morning."

The final snook fishing secret may be the most important.

Yet it's the easiest thing for anglers to do, and the one fishing secret that is most overlooked.

FISHING SECRET NUMBER TEN means keeping a meticulous log book. By keeping a log, then referring to this book, you will begin to understand why something didn't work for you or why it did.

Between your log and this reference book you will begin to understand the snook completely. And understanding this intricate gamefish is important if you want to catch him consistently.

Chapter 14

FLY FISHING FOR SNOOK

One other aspect of the snook's unique life cycle provides a key to consistently catching this gamefish on flies and other small artificial lures.

Like tarpon, juvenile snook penetrate the estuary as far as possible in order to mature in a relatively predator-free environment. These upper reaches of mangrove creeks, drainage ditches, mosquito control ditches and land-locked pond systems often provide the absolute best fishing for snook and small tarpon for the fly rod angler.

Such areas may be partially or totally land-locked. As such they trap snook, tarpon and redfish in the backwaters in big numbers. Meanwhile, these areas don't provide a lot of food for gamefish. And most of the forage that you do find there is small, and just right for "matching the hatch" with flies.

Large snook are notoriously hard to catch on flies. After all, they target large baits like scaled sardines and grunts. So matching that hatch can be difficult. Also large snook have terrific eyesight.

And they arc usually found in bays near passes during the spring and summer. Consequently, big linesiders are often found in crystal clear waters chock full of baitfish. And they easily spot -- and avoid -- a large lure that is worked to simulate a pilchard or grunt.

Small snook are suckers for flies because they are often feeding on fast, darting, small fish like glass minnows. Meanwhile, the land-locked variety feeds predominantly on the fresh and brackish water mosquitofish (gambusia species). These small minnows can be easily simulated by tiny

Good places to catch snook on flies are the same landlocked pond systems that hold baby tarpon like this one.

streamer flies and the fast retrieve they afford means more hookups.

And, while small snook will eagerly gulp tiny flies in the creeks and land-locked ponds, this method of fishing is also a good opportunity for catching a big one on a fly. The larger linesiders often get stuck in these areas. And, in the backwaters, where live pilchards are scarce and the water dirty, big snook bite flies better than just about any other place.

The biggest snook I have ever taken on a fly was a 12-pounder I caught in a land-locked pond. Meanwhile, you can catch dozens of small snook on flies in such locales.

In a scientific study, conducted by Grant Gilmore and his colleagues at the Harbor Branch Oceanographic Institution, juvenile wild snook preferred to eat wild mosquitofish and other small fishes above other prey. Gilmore and company found a different result in stressed conditions -- laboratories where small baitfish can easily avoid predation.

In the labs the little snook ate large food, because they had to. Big baits were much easier to catch then little minnows.

But, in the dirty backwaters, small baits like gambusia, are easy prey for wild snook. And that allows snook to target this food source just as they do glass minnows in open waters. So when snook are feeding on small, fast moving, baitfish they become suckers for flies.

In the chapter on winter fishing we told you how intelligent the snook is. You simply can not show him most baits more than once or twice and expect a hit. So, with flies -- a bait that is normally worked slowly -- the angler has a real problem covering the water. Small flies and fast retrieves, that do not allow the linesider a good look at the bait, are the keys to consistently catching snook in the backwaters where they feed predominantly on such small fish.

But that scenario can change when you fish the spring, summer and fall of the mangrove country. In the murky waters

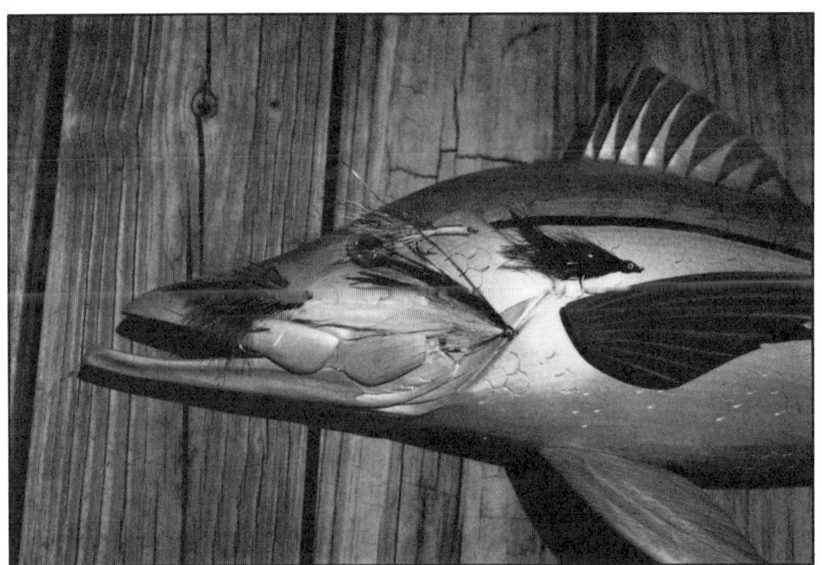

A sculpture of a snook makes an appropriate backdrop for these top snook flies. The Dahlberg Diver is on the nose of the snook, with three top streamer flies on the right.

Flies courtesy of Captain Pete Greenan.

Fly rod snook put on terrific aerial displays with strong runs that rival the traditional king of saltwater fly fishing — the tarpon.

of the 10,000 Islands, lures work well year-round. And many flies that simulate successful snook plugs are deadly.

Jigs are the absolute best lure for catching snook. And fly rodders can simulate this ultimate bait by using copper or lead to weight a bucktail, or by using the weighted eye variety of fly. Whatever the selection, the weighted fly should be used in somewhat deeper waters (experts may use them anywhere) and the fly can be hopped along in quick strips just like a bouncing jig.

The balsa diving lures are famous snook catchers, and one particular fly simulates this lure to perfection. It's called the Dahlberg Diver. It's a tough fly to tie, made of woven and shaved deer body hair. But tossed beneath the mangroves it has few equals in drawing a snook strike.

But -- then -- you still have to get him out from beneath those bushes.

And lure and fly color is more important to snook than any other gamefish. Largemouth bass eat all manner of garish offerings. I've seen blue marlin attempt to eat trolled beer cans. But snook want the colors of the food they are used to.

In clear water green, white and silver colors are the only option if you want to consistently catch snook on flies. In murky seas yellows, browns and blacks are colors that might work. But a plain old white lure will work in just about any

Huge snook can be taken on fly rods during the closed season during the summer. At this time of year they are concentrated in the passes and along the beaches due to spawning season. And the competition and lack of angler pressure can mean boating monsters on flies, though big linesiders are notorious for spurning streamers and their ilk.

water conditions.

For that reason Lefty Kreh's (white) Deceiver may be the best of snook flies. It can be used in clear shallow waters or in the murky creeks. But the Deceiver is followed by two top producers.

Chico Fernandez patterned a Glass Minnow fly that involved green and white bucktail for the tail and also for the wing. Silver mylar wrapped the body of the hook and the mylar was covered by clear monofilament fishing line.

Saint Petersburg Fly Tier Carl Hanson improved on this lure by stringing the white and green bucktail from the hook curve then wrapping the shank in simple tinfoil. Carl covered it with monofilament line as well, but he used a simple nail knot to do it with -- and the thing can be tied by hand in about a minute.

And, while these are the historic patterns that are the original snook flies, today there are hundreds of clones that will work well on snook. Just about any kind of homemade streamer fly makes a good snook lure if the presentation is right and you fish in the proper place.

Weighted lines have little use in snook fly fishing.

Weight the fly instead.

But be on your toes. Snook will often follow a fly and eat it right next to the boat. That's one of the things that makes chasing them with the long wand so rewarding.

You can catch snook on flies during the transitional movement periods, always during the winter months in the backwaters. And they can be taken during the temperate times if they are actively feeding and being chummed with live bait.

Some of the best fly fishing for big snook occurs during the summer in the passes and along the beaches of the west coast. During that time of year the snook's reproductive activities tend to congregate the fish. Consequently, competition for food dramatically increases, and this often offsets the natural wariness of the sharp-eyed linesider.

Scott Moore shows off a fly rod snook.

Scott's biggest fly rod snook was a 24-pound beach fish. But, of course, the summer -- a time when snook are so concentrated -- is also the closed season. And even trophies like that must be released during those months.

Snook, trout and other gamefish are also suckers for flies fished at night beneath the lights, regardless of the time of year.

Still the best time to catch snook on flies is when they are concentrated in semi-land-locked areas. The canals adjacent to Alligator Alley, The Tamiami Trail and the creeks near Goodland are great fly rodding prospects. Along the Atlantic coast a number of impoundment areas provide great fly rodding for both snook and small tarpon.

In fact, any mangrove creek, pond, ditch or stream in snook country may provide terrific fly fishing action. A good way to find fly rod backwater snook is to look for feeding fish -- or rolling small tarpon. Such keys can find you fly rod snook.

The added draw is the shot at fishing's greatest challenge -- fly fishing's grand slam. And that means a snook, tarpon, and redfish on the fly in one trip.

If you fly fish, look to the backwaters. It isn't the only place to get the grand slam, but it's a very good beginning.

Chapter 15

A GUIDE THROUGH SNOOK COOKING

We couldn't let this book go by without a chapter on the eating qualities of the snook. Both authors are known as pretty fair country cooks. And, Scott's background as a former chef for three different restaurants adequately qualifies this fishing guide to instruct anglers in how to prepare tasty dishes of the sumptuous snook that they catch.

But, you don't speak about eating snook lightly. The linesider has been, and still may be in serious trouble. Regulations on the harvest of snook have brought the fish back from the brink of extinction. Yet, the climactic threat that snook face in the U.S. means a constant danger of overfishing this resource.

Consequently, some of Scott's snook recipes have been geared towards utilizing as much of the fish as possible. And that allows more snook dinners, and less fish that have to be killed.

Snook salad came about because of that philosophy. Most anglers throw away the belly meat of the snook rather than deal with the abundant large bones that are found in the belly. Also, the belly meat of most fish is where the majority of the fat is found. So belly meat in many types of fish is oily and of poor quality.

But snook feature extremely lean meat. Like gag or scamp grouper snook is snow white and very firm. And it has very little fat content. Consequently, the belly meat of the snook is delicious, once you separate the meat from the bones.

Many of these recipes utilize as much of the snook as possible in order to conserve this precious resource. In Scott's right hand is the traditional boneless, skinless fillet that make for most recipes. But the other hand holds the belly meat and the throat of the snook — both of these parts of the fish are often discarded. However, the lean snook meat means both the belly and throat can be used for delicious meals.

That's where Scott got the idea of making SNOOK SALAD. For getting the belly meat off the bones involves boiling the bellies then picking the meat away from the bones. So what you end up with is a bunch of small pieces of snook meat similar to the small chunks of tuna that come from a can.

To make snook salad you simply boil the skinless belly meat with a bay leaf or crab and shrimp boiling spices. You can pour some beer or wine into the pot if you want. And snook bellies cook quickly. When the pot comes to a good boil it only takes about five minutes and the fish is done.

After the bellies have cooled the meat is separated from the bones, and you are ready to make snook salad. You make it by adding finely chopped sweet onions (lots) and finely chopped celery to the fish. Mayonnaise and a dash of lemon juice completes the dish. You make snook salad just about the way you do tuna or chicken salad, only don't skip the onion. It really adds to the dish.

I've got a recipe for fried snook that has drawn plenty of raves over the years. In fact, one reader wrote to say she had tried it and it made the best fried fish she had ever tasted. This recipe does involve some advance preparation. I call it MARINATED SNOOK.

To make marinated snook you cut up boneless, skinless snook fillets into frying sized fingers. Put the fingers in a bowl and liberally sprinkle them with black pepper, garlic powder and oregano. Then the snook fingers are covered with a mixture of one third beer, two thirds milk, a couple of eggs (or more, depending on how much snook you are cooking) and enough Worcestershire Sauce to turn the milk/beer mixture golden brown. Flour is also added to this liquid until the mix takes on the consistency of paste.

Now the snook fingers marinate in this for at least four hours, preferably overnight. Consequently, the flour penetrates into the outer tissue of the fish fingers, and that ensures that the fish will seal quickly when it is fried. And that keeps it moist and tender. Meanwhile, the combination of beer, milk, Worcestershire Sauce and the spices adds a unique and complimentary flavor to the fish.

After the fingers have marinated they are drained and

dipped in flour, then fried. And there you have it, marinated snook.

Frying snook that way is quite tasty but it does involve some effort. But Scott has a recipe that is not only delicious but easy as well. It's called ITALIAN BAKED SNOOK.

To make Italian Baked Snook you cut the boneless fillets into large fingers, dip them in a mix of milk and egg and roll them in Italian bread crumbs. The breaded fish are then browned quickly in a skillet with sunflower oil (Scott says the sunflower oil prevents the fish from having a greasy flavor).

The browned fingers are then placed in a greased baking dish and popped into a preheated 325 degree oven. When they flake all the way through (about ten minutes) they are done. This is an easy dish to prepare after a long day on the water.

Because snook are so firm fleshed they are also excellent as a poached fish. To poach snook it isn't necessary to cut them up, unless the fillets are huge. POACHED SNOOK should be left in fillet-sized pieces, though a large pot will be needed.

Into the pot goes crab boil, or bay leaf, white wine, lemon juice and the lemons themselves and salt and pepper. Poaching snook does not mean boiling them. When snook are boiled the meat flakes easily. The goal with poaching is to keep the meat firm. So the pot should never do more than just simmer.

The snook is gently lowered into the simmering pot and the fish is cooked without a lid for about twenty minutes. It's done when it just barely flakes all the way through.

Poached snook is excellent as a cold dish. And this manner of fixing snook lends itself to use with a sauce. The fish can be dipped in cocktail sauce, however, Thousand Island dressing with some lemon juice added also goes well with cold poached snook.

Because snook are so sweet and firm they can also be used over pasta. We have a great recipe called LINGUINE WITH

SNOOK SAUCE that is a big hit, and all you do is substitute chunks of snook for the clams of the traditional dish.

To make Linguine With Snook Sauce you saute chopped garlic, fresh parsley, oregano and marjoram in olive oil. When that's done you add the snook chunks and barely cook them. Then a dash of white wine or sherry is added to the pot. If the dish needs to be thickened flour or corn starch can be mixed into the wine before it is added to the pot.

This stately American egret makes a pretty sight on the gunnel of the Primadonna. But don't turn your back on this thief while cleaning fish, or you might just lose a snook dinner down the bird's gullet. *Photo by Patti Knowles.*

This mixture is then served over Linguine. Keep the parmesan cheese on hand and even the kids will be asking for more.

Snook conservation is becoming more and more important as the number of linesider anglers grows. Yet, snook are in high demand by many gourmets. In reality snook meat is so similar to grouper that 99 percent of the people could never tell the two apart. But you can buy grouper and you can't buy snook, and that has added to the allure of the linesider as an epicurean delight.

As more anglers discover snook fishing the demand for snook by the non-fishing public will also go up. And that is not good for a troubled gamefish that cries out for catch and release fishing. Still there is nothing wrong with eating a few snook. And once again the key here is to use as much of the fish as possible in order to conserve the resource.

And that's where Scott got the idea of eating SNOOK THROATS. Gulf coast anglers have relished eating grouper throats for decades. The throat meat of groupers and other lean fishes is the tastiest part, even though it means a little more work than eating the boneless fillets. And the throats of snook are just as tasty as those of grouper.

To prepare snook throats you have to know how to dress them. The throat must be cut out of the underside of the fish. Snook throats are contained between the pelvic fins on the upper belly of the fish towards the head -- and the gill covers. The throat ends in a narrow V that butts up against the gill plates.

When the throat is cut from the carcass what you end up with is a triangular shaped piece of meat and solid bone, similar to a breast of chicken. Snook throats do not have small bones in them, and the meat can be pulled or chewed from the solid bone just as you would from a fried chicken breast.

Once the throat has been removed from the carcass it can

be easily skinned using a pair of needle nosed pliers to grip the skin and pull it off of the throat. The throat may then be used in any snook recipe.

Fried snook throats are the most popular way of preparing this delicacy. But snook throats also make great seafood chowders as well.

Catch and release fishing for snook is important for preserving snook for the future. But there is no reason the angler can't keep a few snook to eat. After all absolutely fresh fish is one of the treats that only the fishermen can enjoy.

If you eat fish in a restaurant there is no way to tell how fresh it is. But when you caught that snook yourself you are guaranteed of eating the freshest of fish.

And snook are best eaten when they are fresh. So if you want to enjoy them you will have to go fishing for them. And that means learning how to catch them.

RECIPE NOTES:

RECIPE NOTES:

Chapter 16

FUTURE FISHING: WHERE & HOW?

The snook has survived some terrific adventures for a gamefish. From the ancient migrations during prehistory to the snook's unique adaptation to life in a place where it simply does not belong, the linesider is a rare creature.

But the troubles and travails of the centropomus tribe didn't stop in prehistory. Freezes and red tides have almost ended the snook's existence in the U.S. during the memory of modern man. Through DNA testing Mike Tringali of the Florida Department of Natural Resources has documented some great calamity that befell the snook population of Tampa Bay -- some disaster that these snook, at the northern limit of their range, still have not recovered from.

Sophisticated DNA testing shows that these snook are interbreeding, thus suggesting a large population crash at some time in the past. It could have been the killer freezes of the 1960's, or the 18-month long red tide in the 1840's. Or it could have been any of a number of killer hurricanes that have visited Tampa Bay in modern history or before humans recorded such events. Or it could have been a series of such disasters.

So the story of the snook is an ongoing one. And therein lies the future of these fish. As this book goes to press a move is on to ban the majority of commercial fishing nets from inshore waters in Florida. Such a ban is already in effect in many coastal states. And such controls should help the snook population, as well as the populations of all fish.

Meanwhile, snook were rescued from the ravages of legal

commercial exploitation during the 1950's. And while a black market in snook fillets still operates, the poaching of this great gamefish has dwindled from its heyday in the 1960's and 70's.

But legal recreational harvest of snook has soared as Scott Moore showed anglers, and the guides who followed him, how to catch these gamesters. Consequently, today's snook sees more legal pressure on him and less illegal harvest.

Still, legal harvest can and is being controlled. Strict limits and season closures have all helped the snook population rebound significantly from the crisis of the early 1980's

FDNR scientists have calculated that the snook population in the Port Manatee region of Tampa Bay doubled between 1990 and 1992. Yet those were years with warm winters. And snook are so dependent on environmental factors that such a population increase should be viewed with caution.

But things are looking up for the snook with one exception. Snook mean grant money and fame for scientists. So the amount of scientific research being done on snook has increased 50-fold in the last decade. And the more we know about these unique gamefish the more we will be able to protect them in the future.

One notable debacle in the realm of science has been the utter failure of several scientific attempts to rear snook in hatcheries in order to replenish wild snook populations. Phil Chapman and Paul Shafland of the Florida Game and Freshwater Fish Commission remain the only scientists to succeed in an artificial stocking program involving snook. A multi-million dollar FDNR snook hatchery at Port Manatee has yet to approach success in rearing snook artificially. But there has been a change in management there, and perhaps this facility may become more successful in the future.

There is still hope in this area. Dr. Randy Edwards, a pioneer snook hatchery researcher, has raised snook in the laboratory at Mote Marine Laboratory. And Edwards -- without fanfare -- has been one of a handful of scientists to put some snook

One great need for the endangered snook is a successful artificial hatchery program. Phil Chapman of the Florida Game and Freshwater Fish Commission remains the only scientist to perform that feat. Chapman reared this finglerling in the 1970s as part of a program to introduce snook into freshwater lakes. Similiar programs are planned for the state of Texas at this time.

back into the wild.

Perhaps it's time to take artificial snook propagation out of the hands of governmental agencies and allow private enterprise to have a greater role in that endeavor. Hopefully, the shakeup in FDNR management will lead to better interagency cooperation in the hatchery business.

But hatcheries are only a small part of what's needed to perpetuate healthy populations of snook. Habitat degradation remains the chief villain for all wildlife. And there are folks working on those problems.

Wanton destruction of mangroves, grass flats and salt marshes is increasingly becoming a thing of the past in the U.S. -- even with Florida's burgeoning human population. Meanwhile, people like scientist Mike Calinski are designing

With more regulations and information on snook the future for this gamefish looks bright. But the linesider is still subject to threats.

artificial habitats as nursery areas for snook and other gamefish. And some of the destructive devices of the past may actually help a unique animal like the snook.

When unknowing bureaucrats dug mosquito control ditches that degraded the natural habitat of Florida during the 1930's, 40's and 50's they may have actually aided the snook. Such ditches afford predator-free environments for young snook. And they also provide warmth and protection from winter's cold. Such artificial backwaters may eventually allow the snook population to expand, because such sheltered canals are much closer to abundant food sources than the snook's traditional wintering grounds far up the rivers.

The same thing can be said for the warm water runoffs from power plants along both Florida coasts. Such warm water refuges may mean more food for wintering snook, and that could translate into population increases.

And that's where the better fishing will be. Snook are not

overly complicated. They go where the food, weather and least amount of danger can be found.

Mild winters and the absence of a commercial purse seine fishery north of Saint Petersburg has resulted in the terrific "new" fishery at Honeymoon Island and around the Anclote and Pithlachascotee Rivers.

Meanwhile, a partial ban on the purse seining of baitfish in Tampa Bay in 1992 has seen the snook population soar there as well. Most of the snook are small in Tampa Bay. But there are plenty of them now that a threat to their chief food source has been curtailed.

In Charlotte Harbor and points south purse seining of bait has never been as intense as it is further north. And that's probably because migratory baitfish are not nearly as abundant in that area. Yet, because of the somewhat milder winters in southwest Florida, the snook are not nearly as dependent on the migratory bait as they are further north. Charlotte Harbor snook tend to eat shrimp, mutton minnows and other baits while the snook of Tampa Bay want only scaled sardines.

The east coast has always had good snook populations. Two factors benefit the snook of the Atlantic Ocean. First the proximity of the Gulf Stream means warmer waters for east coast snook during the winter. Meanwhile east coast snook have the benefit of a lee shore during the northwest winds brought on by winter cold fronts.

Such protection from the cold has been the primary reason for the success of the snook in the Atlantic. East coast snook do not have to flee into river systems that are practically devoid of food in order to escape killer freezes. Consequently, they don't face near-starvation during the winter like the snook of the gulfcoast.

Therefore, east coast snook have not had to depend on the reliability of one particular food source (the scaled sardine) the way the snook of the gulf have. Hence, east coast snook have become more versatile in food targeting. They have much less total dependency on the influx of whitebait into the estuary and have habits more like the snook of tropical regions.

East coast snook do depend on the whitebait migration. It's the primary reason they gang up in the inlets along the Atlantic Ocean. And more east coast anglers should use pilchards for snook bait. But east coast snook are not nearly as dependent on that one specific food source as their gulfcoast brethren.

The future looks good for snook. But there are problems as well. Ospreys take their toll, sharks and dolphins eat snook. And there is always the threat of a freeze.

Photo by Captain Van Hubbard.

Reduced sheetwater flow, pollution, drainage and the other environmental disasters visited on the Everglades and Florida Bay during the last century have certainly changed things in south Florida. And while coral reefs and sawgrass may be dying, something has happened in the last decade to swell the population of snook in the Florida Keys.

Keys skiff guides who once guided their clients to catches of bonefish, tarpon and permit now do a brisk business in snook. The linesiders don't have to go upriver in the sunny keys. And pilchards spend their winters prowling the grass flats adjacent to that part of Florida.

So the future of snook looks bright, though it is subject to abrupt change. Florida is overdue for a killer freeze and a bad red tide. And the west coast is way overdue for a killer hurricane. Andrew was a tiny thing compared to the blow of 1848.

But we have the mechanics in place to protect the snook from such calamities now. Further regulations are planned that would control the harvest of all inshore marine life. And such sweeping conservation moves can only help the snook.

So the best fishing will be the places where the least pressure is put on the snook. The spot where baitfish are plentiful. And in the right weather conditions. And all of those things can change from hour to hour.

That's snook fishing. There is no set formula for success. But, by knowing what you now know about snook, you can alter fishing styles as the snook alters his way as well.

Snook spell adventure, by their very nature. And snook fishing provides one of life's great adventures for we members of the human race.

Join us on the water sometime, and you'll see what we mean.

ORDER FORM

I would like to order additional copies of **Captain Scott Moore's Snook Fishing Secrets**.

Please mail __________ copies to the address below:

NAME ____

ADDRESS ____

CITY ____________________ STATE ________ ZIP ____________

Number of books being ordered _______ x $14.95 per book = TOTAL AMOUNT ENCLOSED (Check or Money Order)

$________________

Price includes postage and handling.

Please mail your check or money order to:

SEVEN PINES PUBLISHING CO.
P.O. Box 14069
Bradenton, FL 34280-4069

Thanks and good fishing!

Here's what the critics say about Captain Scott Moore's Snook Fishing Secrets...

Capt. Scott Moore, one of Florida's top snook guides for many years, has teamed up with outdoor writer G.B. Knowles to produce what could be the definitive work on how, where, and when to catch Florida snook.

—Saltwater Sportsman Magazine

Not only is this book the most definitive work to date on the snook, but it is full of fishing tips that will teach the reader how to work the Scott Moore magic on any species of fish in fresh or saltwater.

—Southeastern Outdoor Press Association News

Moore is widely recognized as an outstanding snook guide, and many of his theories are original.

—Byron Stout, Fort Myers News-Press

In addition to solid "how-to" fishing information, this book provides a fascinating look at the life cycle of the snook and evolution of modern snook fishing.

—Tim Tucker, The Gainseville Sun

No species of fish in our watery world is more mysterious or misunderstood than the snook, and seldom does a book come along that gives the wealth of information as does G.B. Knowles' *Captain Scott Moore's Snook Fishing Secrets.*

—The Longboat Key Observer Newspaper

Moore and writer G.B. Knowles have teamed up to produce a book on snook fishing tricks and methods that can be adapted anywhere in the state.

—Bill Sargent, Florida Today

In their first venture into the publishing world, Knowles and Moore landed a lunker; one that won't be thrown back by Florida anglers. The book is a trophy that will be consumed for years to come.

—Steve Gibson, Sarasota Herald Tribune

Captain Scott Moore's Snook Fishing Secrets is arranged in chapters that will allow quick browsing for use as a reference book. Yet its narrative style weaves a fascinating story about snook and snook fishing. And the book is full of instructive photographs that will visually guide the reader to understanding how to catch this most popular of saltwater gamefish.

—The Dolphin Newspaper

It's no longer possible for the average weekend fisherman to charter Moore most of the year. He has been so successful that his regular customers keep him booked years in advance, with some taking a particular week each year, others opting for one day per week almost year around.

But the book offers a close look at Moore's tactics, revealed by the guy who probably knows him better than anyone except his wife. It's an education, even for an experienced snooker.

—Frank Sargeant, Tampa Tribune

Of all the information spread throughout the book, I found the chapter on *Ten Fishing Secrets* to hold some of the best snook fishing information currently available in print. From how wind direction effects fishing to understanding the solunar periods and moon phases and using them to catch snook and baitfish, each tip displays an insight into snook fishing that has taken years of observation for Moore to conceive and develop.

—Mike Holliday, Port St. Lucie Tribune

The book is a 176-page epic that will have rank-and-file anglers, fishing writers and outdoor enthusiasts entranced.

—Marilyn Hoeckel, Boca Beacon

In angling circles, it's almost universally conceded—there's Capt. Scott Moore—then everyone else.

—The Suncoast News

Of course, Capt. Scott Moore's snook book is a great gift. It's well worth reading, and I feel everyone can learn something from it.

Please notice Capt. Scott's sincere desire to promote conservation and protect these beautiful, valuable fish that we are privileged to share.

—Capt. Van Hubbard, Boca Beacon

Part of the reason Knowles thinks Moore is such a good angler is that he's hyperactive—always moving. When Moore started, there were only about 30 people who knew how to do inshore snook guiding, Knowles said. Now there are hundreds. "He really created the inshore guiding industry on the west coast of Florida, even the east coast," Knowles said.

—Gasparilla Gazette

Knowles' chronicle of Moore's fishing career has fanned the legend. The two friends collaborated on a book called *Captain Scott Moore's Snook Fishing Secrets.*

"Scott is generally acknowledged as an expert when it comes to catching snook," Knowles says. "Scott is to snook fishing as Dan Marino is to throwing a football."

—Carlos Galarza, Bradenton Herald

LOG ENTRIES: